The Understanding Your Grief

Support Group Guide

D1304684

Also by Alan Wolfelt

Eight Critical Questions for Mourners...
And the Answers That Will Help You Heal

Healing Your Grieving Heart:
100 Practical Ideas

Healing A Friend's Grieving Heart:
100 Practical Ideas for Helping Someone You Love Through Loss

The Journey Through Grief:
Reflections on Healing

Understanding Your Grief:
Ten Essential Touchstones for Finding Hope
and Healing Your Heart

The Understanding Your Grief Journal:
Exploring the Ten Essential Touchstones

The Understanding Your Grief
Support Group Guide
Starting and Leading a
Bereavement Support Group

A companion guide for support group leaders
for use with *Understanding Your Grief* and
The Understanding Your Grief Journal

Alan D. Wolfelt, Ph.D.

Companion Press is an imprint of the
Center for Loss and Life Transition
3735 Broken Bow Road
Fort Collins, Colorado 80526.

Printed in the United States of America

17 16 15 14 13 12   6 5 4 3

ISBN: 978-1-879651-40-1

Companion
P R E S S

*Companion Press is dedicated to the education and support of both the
bereaved and bereavement caregivers. We believe that those who companion
the bereaved by walking with them as they journey in grief have a wondrous
opportunity: to help others embrace and grow through grief—and to lead
fuller, more deeply-lived lives themselves because of this important ministry.*

For a complete catalog and ordering information,
write or call:

Companion Press
The Center for Loss and Life Transition
3735 Broken Bow Road
Fort Collins, CO 80526
(970) 226-6050
www.centerforloss.com

Contents

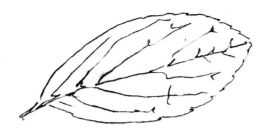

Introduction
In Gratitude to the Grief Support Group Facilitator

If you hope to support other people in their grief journeys and are planning to use this support group guide in conjunction with the *Understanding Your Grief* book and journal, let me begin by thanking you.

Grief, often the most profound form of sorrow, demands the support and compassion of our fellow human beings. Since the beginning of time, people have come together in times of grief to help one another. Grief support groups provide an opportunity for this kind of help and support. Again, thank you for your efforts to help create a "safe place" to nurture others. When you are privileged to witness the pain soften and hope emerge, you realize it is worth all your efforts.

Yes, starting and leading a grief support group is not only worth the effort, it is enriching and rewarding. My thirty years of experience in "companioning" people in grief have taught me that it is a true privilege to "walk with" and learn from my fellow travelers. They have taught me so much about individual and group support. Now, a vital part of the mission of my Center for Loss and Life Transition is to give back what I have learned.

The Medical Model of Bereavement Care

One important thing I have learned is that much of what I was taught about grief while I was earning my doctorate in psychology was too rooted in the medical model of caregiving. Like me, many mental health caregivers were trained in this model. They were taught that grief, like other psychological troubles, could be considered an illness that needs proper assessment and diagnosis and, with treatment, can be "cured."

I believe the limitations of our clinical, medical models are profound and far-reaching. Our modern understanding of grief all too often projects that for "successful" mourning to take place, the person must disengage from the person who died and, by all means, "let go." We even have all sorts of books full of techniques on how to help others "let go" or reach "closure."

Our modern understanding of grief often urges the bereaved (which means "to be torn apart," "to have special needs") to deny any form of continued relationship with the person who died. For many, the hallmark of so-called "pathological grief" has been the continued relationship the mourner feels between him or herself and the person who died.

Our modern understanding of grief all too often conveys that the end result of bereavement is a series of completed tasks, extinguished pain, and the establishment of new relationships. In attempting to make a science of grief, we have compartmentalized complex emotions with neat clinical labels.

Our modern understanding of grief all too often uses a "recovery" or "resolution" definition to suggest a return to "normalcy." Recovery, as understood by some, mourners and caregivers alike, is erroneously seen as an absolute, a perfect state of reestablishment.

Our modern understanding of grief for some is based on the model of crisis theory that purports that a person's life is in a state of homeostatic balance, then something comes along (like death) and knocks the person out of balance. Caregivers are taught intervention goals to reestablish the prior state of homeostasis. There is only one major problem with this theory—it doesn't work. Why? Because a person's life is changed forever after the death of someone loved.

Our modern understanding of grief all too often pathologizes others' experiences with disregard for cultural and personality differences. (For example, keening is legitimized in some cultures and is seen as abnormal in others. Gotta watch where you keen; you may be hospitalized.)

Our modern understanding of grief all too often lacks any appreciation for and attention to the spiritual nature of the grief journey. As authors such as Frankl, Fromm, and Jung noted years ago, and Hillman more recently, academic psychology has been too interfaced with the natural sciences and laboratory methods of weighing, counting, and objective reporting. Some of us, often through no fault of our own, but perhaps by the contamination of our formal training, have overlooked the journey into grief as a soul-based journey.

If you are a layperson who will be leading a bereavement support group, you may also have been affected by the medical model of bereavement care. Have you absorbed our culture's judgments that it is wrong to cry in public, that the person who died wouldn't want us to be sad, that mourners need to find ways to "get over" their grief? These myths are in part an outgrowth of the dominant (and harmful) medical model of bereavement care.

The Art of Companioning

The word "treat" comes from the Latin root word "tractare," which means "to drag." If we combine that with "patient" we can really get in trouble. "Patient" means "passive long-term sufferer," so if we treat patients, we drag passive long-term sufferers. (Doesn't sound very empowering to me.)

Instead of the medical model of bereavement caregiving, I support a more soulful, holistic model of what it means to help someone in grief. I call it my "companioning" model of bereavement care.

The word "companion," when broken down into its original Latin roots means "messmate": *com* for "with" and *pan* for "bread." Someone you would share a meal with, a friend, an equal. I have taken liberties with the noun "companion" and made it into the verb "companioning" because it so well captures the type of counseling relationship I advocate.

3

More specifically, for me . . .

- Companioning is about honoring the spirit; it is not about focusing on the intellect.
- Companioning is about curiosity; it is not about expertise.
- Companioning is about learning from others; it is not about teaching them.
- Companioning is about walking alongside; it is not about leading.
- Companioning is about being still; it is not about frantic movement forward.
- Companioning is about discovering the gifts of sacred silence; it is not about filling every painful moment with words.
- Companioning is about listening with the heart; it is not about analyzing with the head.
- Companioning is about bearing witness to the struggles of others; it is not about directing those struggles.
- Companioning is about being present to another person's pain; it is not about taking away the pain.
- Companioning is about respecting disorder and confusion; it is not about imposing order and logic.
- Companioning is about going to the wilderness of the soul with another human being; it is not about thinking you are responsible for finding the way out.

Yes, the grief journey requires contemplation and turning inward. In other words, it requires depression, anxiety, and loss of control. It requires going to the wilderness. Quietness and emptiness invite the heart to observe signs of sacredness, to regain purpose, to rediscover love, to renew life! Searching for meaning, reasons to get one's feet out of bed, and understanding the pain of loss are not the domain of the medical model of bereavement care. Experience has taught me that it is the mysterious, spiritual dimension of grief that harbors the capacity to go on living until we, too, die.

I encourage you to hold the companioning philosophy of bereavement care in your heart as you support your group members.

The Myth of the Expert in Grief

There is a Buddhist teaching that says, "In the beginner's mind there are many possibilities; in the expert's mind there are few." Let's explore the consequences when others, such as your group members, think of you as leader as an "expert."

In his lovely book *Improvisational Therapy* (1990), Bradford P. Kenney writes brilliantly about the hazards of being considered an "expert" or "master" counselor:

> *You will find that it no longer matters what you say. Everything uttered will be contextualized as the voice of a master. A casual handshake will be taken as a trance induction. A belch becomes a brilliant intervention. The snoring in a nap becomes the voice of therapeutic wisdom.*
>
> *Avoid the political posturings of "mastery" and return to embracing and cultivating a beginner's mind. Maintain and respect ignorance. Speak to hear the surprise from your own voice.*

As you contemplate the risk of being an expert, listen to your own inner voice. What has your personal grief taught you about what helps people heal? What have grieving people taught you? What are your own personal strengths and limitations as a caregiver? Are you an open learner who is willing to be taught, or are you an expert who treats people like patients?

Many of you are not certified grief educators, counselors, or therapists. That doesn't mean, however, you aren't resourceful, talented, compassionate people who can help people heal in grief. I encourage you to join us certified grief counselors and therapists, and to pursue your professional development—while at the same time not striving to be an "expert." Certification is not an end-stage of counselor development. Continual professional development and openness to learning new tools and "ways of being" are essential for each of us.

As caregivers to people in grief, I believe we would be well-served to discover our own "self-as-instrument." It was Combs who years ago introduced the concept of "self-as-instrument" to the counseling literature.

He warned against the strict adherence to a particular model or school of counseling and essentially urged caregivers to discover their unique gifts and make use of them. He warned that we shouldn't become counselors cloned in the image of others, but instead strive to awaken, cultivate, and nurture imagination and creativity in ourselves, in our colleagues, and in our clients.

I believe that counseling people in grief—as well as leading grief support groups—is more of an art than a science. An artist fully embraces his or her personal strengths and limitations to evolve a unique style that becomes a self-portrait as a counselor and as a human being.

Using the Support Group Guide

This support group guide is to help you get started with and provide effective leadership to your grief support group. The contents cover a variety of important topics, from planning group meetings to responding to potential problems in the group and evaluating your group's progress. Those of you familiar with my previous writings may recognize some of the content targeted at support group leadership. Here it is updated, and I hope you will also find the new 12-session meeting plan using *Understanding Your Grief* to be of help to you as you reach out to minister to those in need of a meaningful group experience.

Please note that to use the 12-session plan, each of your group members will need to obtain both *Understanding Your Grief* and *The Understanding Your Grief Journal*. They are available through bookstores or as a two-volume, discounted set on my website: www.centerforloss.com. (Also see the Bereavement Support Group Start-Up Package advertised at the back of this book.)

You and the bereaved people you will go on to help will be held in my thoughts and prayers. Grieving people need to know they are not alone—that there are safe places and kind and loving people willing to help them. Even in the wilderness of grief, they can reach out and discover comfort and support. Most of all, they can discover there is hope for tomorrow. These are the critical ingredients for healing.

Best wishes as you companion those who mourn.

Sincerely,

Alan D. Wolfelt

Alan D. Wolfelt, Ph.D.
Director, Center for Loss and Life Transition

Growing Through Grief
The Role of Support Groups

The quality and quantity of understanding support you get during your work of mourning will have a major influence on your capacity to heal. You cannot — nor should you try to — do this alone. Drawing on the experiences and encouragement of friends and fellow grievers is not a weakness but a healthy human need.

Alan Wolfelt, *Understanding Your Grief*

There is a growing realization among those who care for mourners that support groups are an appropriate and effective way to help bereaved people heal. Because they offer a safe place for people to do the work of mourning, support groups encourage participants to reconcile their losses and go on to find continued meaning in life and living. Attending a support group facilitated by a skilled leader often brings comfort and understanding beyond many people's expectations.

Support groups help grieving people by:

- introducing them to others who have had similar experiences, thoughts, and feelings.
- countering the sense of isolation that many experience in our shame-based, mourning-avoiding culture.
- providing emotional, physical, and spiritual support in a safe, nonjudgmental environment.

- allowing them to explore their many thoughts and feelings about grief in a way that helps them be compassionate with themselves.
- encouraging members to not only receive support and understanding for themselves, but also to provide the same to others.
- offering opportunities to learn new ways of approaching problems (e.g., the friend or in-law who lacks an understanding of the need to mourn and pushes you to "return to normal").
- helping them trust their fellow human beings and bond again in what for many in grief feels like an unsafe, uncaring world.
- giving them a forum to search for meaning in life and death.
- providing a supportive environment that can reawaken their zest for life and give them hope for healing.

In short, as group members give and receive help, they feel less helpless and are able to discover continued meaning in life. Feeling understood by others brings down barriers between mourners and the world outside. This process of being understood is central to being compassionate with oneself as a bereaved person. The more people are compassionate to mourners from the outside in, the more mourners are capable of being self-compassionate from the inside out.

Our mourning-avoiding culture often forces bereaved people to withdraw from insensitive friends and family or to adopt ways of avoiding the painful, but necessary, work of mourning; support groups, which instead foster the experience of trusting and being trusted, can do wonders in meeting the needs of bereaved people. In an effective grief support group, members can achieve a balance between giving and receiving, between independence and an appropriate, self-sustaining dependence. The group provides a safe harbor where hurting people can pull in, anchor while the wind still blows them around, and search for safe ground on which to go on living. As a potential leader of such a group, you have the honor of accompanying people during this time.

Before we go on to explore the specifics of running a bereavement support group, though, I would like to further define what I mean by growing through grief.

Growth means encountering pain
The death of someone loved naturally brings about emotional, physical, and spiritual pain for us as human beings. Forums such as support groups provide us with a safe place where we can embrace our pain in "doses." Encountering the pain of the loss all at once would overwhelm us and leave us defenseless. Sometimes bereaved people need to distract themselves from the pain of the loss, while at other times they need a "safe harbor" to pull into and embrace the depth of the loss.

Growth means change
My experience has taught me that we as human beings are forever changed by the death of someone in our lives. To "resolve" your own or someone else's grief often denotes a return to a homeostasis (inner balance) that was present prior to the death. I believe this model of care is inadequate and often damaging to mourners of all ages.

A "return to inner balance" doesn't reflect how I, or the people who have taught me about their grief journeys, are forever changed by the experience of bereavement. In using the word growth, I acknowledge the changes that mourning brings about.

Growth means a new inner balance with no end points
While the bereaved person may do the work of mourning to recapture in part some sense of inner balance, it is a new inner balance. My hope is that the term growth reflects the active, ongoing process of mourning.

Growth means exploring our assumptions about life
The encounter with grief reawakens us to the importance of utilizing our potentials. The concept of potential in this context could be defined as our capacity to mourn our losses openly and without shame, to be interpersonally effective in our relationships with others, and to continue to discover fulfillment in life, living, and loving. Loss often serves as a catalyst to becoming more of what we can be instead of staying exactly what and where we are. Loss seems to free the potential within. Then, it becomes up to us as human beings to embrace and creatively express this potential. Growth is about not settling for homeostasis, but looking for and seeking out how we are changed by this death. Growth means discovering our gifts, our potentials, and using them to bring meaning to the lives of others.

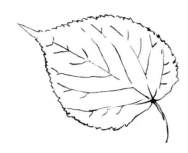

Getting Started
The Nuts and Bolts

Starting a support group can take a lot of time and energy. In fact, I have seen many counselors decide not to start groups simply because they foresaw too many roadblocks and details to attend to. But let me tell you a little secret: even though you will be group leader, you needn't do everything yourself! Instead, round up other interested community members to help you with the start-up activities. A committee of compassionate professionals and bereaved people can share the workload and, even more important, can bring a variety of valuable ideas to the process.

As you complete them, check off the following start-up tasks:

_____ **Performing a needs assessment**

Before your commendable enthusiasm causes you to plunge headlong into running your support group, step back and formally assess the interest in grief support groups in your community. Questions to address include: What kind of grief support groups already exist in this community? What has been the history and success of these groups? What have the leaders of these groups learned about what works and what doesn't here? Are there enough people interested in being group members? Who else is willing to commit time and effort to make this group successful?

Notes

_____

_____

_____

_____ Deciding on a group format

What kind of support group will you provide? Many support groups combine education with support and may be facilitated by either a trained layperson or a professional counselor. Self-help groups (which may or may not be affiliated with a national organization, such as The Compassionate Friends) are led by bereaved people who have already worked toward reconciliation of the death of someone loved. Therapy support groups are led by professional therapists and are limited to a small number of members. Social support groups are usually intended for people who have already worked toward reconciliation of the death of someone loved, but who would benefit from social contact with people who share their experiences.

You also must decide who will join your group. Will the group be homogenous—made up of people who have experienced a specific type of loss (e.g. SIDS, homicide, long-term illness) or will their common bond simply be that each group member has had someone loved die? In homogenous groups, the similarity of losses often creates a tremendous bond for members and makes relating to each other very easy. However, depending on the size of your community, you may or may not be able to achieve this homogeneity. In small communities, you may need to intermix mourners with different loss histories. The main thing to avoid is having someone feel so different from other group members that he or she feels alone and isolated.

Notes

_____

_____

_____

_____ Finding a compatible co-leader

While you may choose to lead this support group by yourself, there are a number of good reasons to have a co-leader. First, leading a support group can be a lot of work. Having two people to plan meetings and lead discussions splits the burden. It also gives you someone to bounce ideas off and de-brief with after meetings. If there is a problem in the group, your co-leader can help solve the problem. If you are sick one week, instead of canceling the meeting as you would have to do if you were the only leader, your co-leader can probably manage without you. Just be certain to find someone with a similar philosophy about grief and a compatible personality.

Notes

_____

_____

_____

_____

_____ Finding and preparing a meeting place

Obviously, you hope to find a comfortable, safe place to hold your group meetings. Public buildings such as libraries, schools, churches, and community centers usually provide rooms free of charge. Try to select a room appropriate for creating a supportive atmosphere, neither too large nor too small and preferably distraction-free. A room without telephones but away from heavy traffic areas is best. Also, pay attention to both the height of the ceiling and the lighting. Very high ceilings often make for a lack of intimacy. Lamps that provide soft lighting are preferable to bright overhead lights. A large chalkboard is handy for many of the meeting activities. You may also want to consider bringing a small boombox or portable stereo and playing soft, appropriate music as people are gathering. And bring simple snacks, or have members sign up to provide them. Having food on hand helps people feel welcome and convivial. Consider taking a short snack break between the education part of the meeting and the open, unstructured sharing part.

Notes

_____

_____

_____

_____

_____ Setting the number of participants

The number of support group members will be related to the kind and quality of interaction you desire. When groups get too large, the sense of safety and freedom to be verbally expressive diminishes for many people. For involved interaction, try to limit your group to no more than 12 members.

Notes

_____

_____

_____

_____

_____ Establishing the structure of the group

You must also determine the structure of the support group. Will it be "open-ended," meaning that group members come and go depending on their needs? Or will it be "closed-ended," meaning that the group will meet for a specific number of days or weeks? In my experience, members feel more comfortable knowing specifically when the group will begin and when it will end.

Notes

_____

_____

_____

_____

_____ Determining length and frequency of meetings

My experience suggests that grief support groups for adults work best when each meeting runs 90 minutes to two hours. Obviously, some of your length considerations will have to do with the number of participants you have; so that everyone has a chance to talk, larger groups demand longer group meetings.

Some groups meet weekly, some bi-weekly, some monthly. However, you should be creative in determining which length and frequency will work best for your unique group and your unique community. The meeting plans outlined in this book are intended for a group that meets weekly for 12 consecutive weeks.

Notes

_____

_____

_____

_____

_____

_____

_____ Pre-screening group members

Not every grieving person makes a good support group member. People with extensive complication of the grief journey or long histories of serious emotional problems are generally better helped by individual counseling (see the Red Flags on p. 76). This will be a judgment call on your part, so don't punish yourself if you occasionally admit someone to a group whom you later determine would be better served elsewhere.

How do you pre-screen? If time permits, I recommend you conduct brief, one-on-one meetings with potential group members before the group begins. Or, sometimes a quick phone conversation will tell you what you need to know. The third alternative is to see how the first group meeting goes then privately screen out those whose grief journeys make them more likely candidates for individual counseling. With this last method, however, you risk alienating group members from the start if one among them behaves inappropriately during the first meeting.

While screening, you also want to pay attention to the recency of the loss. I have found that while there are always exceptions, most people are not ready for a support group experience until at least three months after the death of someone loved. In fact, mourners are typically more responsive to group support approximately five to seven months after the death. On the other hand, don't shame anyone who has had a very recent loss and wants to join your support group. Sometimes acute mourners desperately need the lifeline a grief group can provide. Don't set rigid parameters here; use your best judgment.

Notes

_____

_____

_____

_____

_____

What If I Miss?
What to do if a group member's needs are too great

Even if you've done a good job pre-screening group members, once in awhile it will turn out that a participant isn't suited to your group. If this has happened to you, go easy on yourself! I've been pre-screening and doing grief groups for many years, and I "miss" sometimes, too!

When you discover there is a mismatch between a participant's needs and the group's ability to help, you have an ethical responsibility to refer the person to other sources of support and care. This happens when a participant has serious complications in their grief and the group attempts to provide all the care he or she needs. This can result in the group spending the bulk of its time on one member's needs, to the exclusion of everyone else. I have witnessed grief groups that attempt to carry a load of care that is so large it destroys the entire group.

Don't try to care for someone in your group who really needs individual, professional counseling. When a group leader tries to provide that kind of care in the group setting, it serves neither the complicated mourner nor the rest of the group.

In these cases, be prepared to make an appropriate referral. Often the complicated mourner knows on some level that he needs more help and is grateful. Be sure you are knowledgeable about your community's therapists and their areas of specialty. You'll want to make referrals to a counselor with experience in companioning mourners with death loss.

Sample Support Group Ground Rules

1. *Each person's grief is unique.* While you may share some commonalities in your experiences, no two of you are exactly alike. Consequently, respect and accept both what you have in common with others and what is unique to each of you.

2. *Grief is not a disease, and no "quick-fix" exists for what you are feeling.* Don't set a specific timetable for how long it should take you or others to heal.

3. *Feel free to talk about your grief.* However, if someone in the group decides to listen without sharing, please respect his or her preference.

4. *There is a difference between actively listening to what another person is saying and expressing your own grief.* Make every effort not to interrupt when someone else is speaking.

5. *Thoughts, feelings, and experiences shared in this group will stay in this group.* Respect others' right to confidentiality. Do not use names of fellow participants in discussions outside the group.

6. *Allow each person equal time to express himself or herself* so a few people don't monopolize the group's time.

7. *Attend each group meeting and be on time.* If you decide to leave the group before this series of meetings is completed, be willing to discuss your decision with the group.

8. *Avoid "advice giving" unless it is specifically requested by a group member.* If advice is not solicited, don't give it. If a group member poses a question, share ideas that helped you if you experienced a similar situation. Remember that this group is for support, not therapy.

9. *Recognize that thoughts and feelings are neither right nor wrong.* Enter into the thoughts and feelings of other group members without trying to change them.

10. *Create an atmosphere of willing, invited sharing.* If you feel pressured to talk but don't want to, say so. Your right to quiet contemplation will be respected by the group.

_____ Creating group ground rules

Through appropriately pre-screening participants and establishing group ground rules, you can create a safe place for people to mourn. Ground rules are also important to your role as a leader. For example, should someone begin to verbally dominate the group, you can intervene by pointing out a ground rule that ensures members will have equal time to express themselves. I suggest you distribute copies of your group's ground rules to all members during the first session. You might also want to post them in your meeting room.

See the sample ground rules on page 18 for suggestions.

Notes

_____

_____

_____

_____

_____ Publicizing your group

Since support groups are generally non-profit organizations, free publicity is yours for the asking. Try any or all of the following venues:

Local newspapers
Most have community calendars that will announce your group and publish its upcoming schedule for free. You might also check with the features editor about running a short article on your group.

Radio/TV stations
Write a press release and send it to your local media.

Posters/Flyers
Post them on bulletin boards around town. Be sure to mail to funeral homes,   churches, hospices, hospitals, and area counseling agencies.

Phone calls/Personal contact
Don't neglect to call or even meet with those who are in a position to publicize your group: clergy, healthcare professionals, funeral directors, etc.

Word of mouth
Perhaps your best source of publicity is the "word of mouth" referrals that will begin to spread from graduates of your groups. Encourage your group graduates to keep an eye out for other people in grief whom they can refer to your group.

Notes

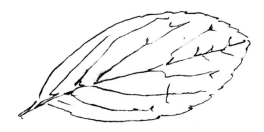

How to Lead
Tasks, Qualities, and Skills of an Effective Leader

A support group leader serves the group by enabling members to achieve the purpose of the support group. That purpose is generally to create a safe place for people to do the work of mourning in a way that allows them to reconcile the loss and go on to find continued meaning in life and living. Sensitive, skilled leadership is often a vital link to a group's fulfillment of its goals.

Obviously, your specific support group may have varying purposes and goals that guide its existence. No matter the goals, however, the group leader's responsibilities remain largely the same. They are responsible for assisting the group in:

- determining the group's purpose.
- outlining the group's structure and length.
- pre-screening potential members.
- clarifying expectations and assisting in the development of group ground rules.
- organizing details.

Now let's explore some of the specific tasks that are often a part of a bereavement support group leader's job description. Again, keep in mind that every group has its own unique requirements.

- *Articulating a guiding philosophy*: Identifying the basic tenets (theoretical orientation) that guide your "way of being" and providing a rationale for any skills or techniques you make use of in group.

- *Planning and leading group meetings*: Preparing for, organizing, and facilitating the group meetings.

- *Listening*: To model and to be an effective listener, you must really hear and allow participants to "teach you" and each other what they are thinking and feeling.

- *Understanding and facilitating group process*: Having knowledge of and being skilled in facilitating group process. (I cannot emphasize enough the importance of leaders getting some fundamental training, not only in the grief process, but also in group process.)

- *Modeling openness and caring*: Providing a role model by being warm, caring, and empathetic and by consciously seeking ways to help the group achieve its purpose.

- *Remaining flexible*: Having an awareness of the need to modify the group activities and skills to fit the unique needs of a specific group or a specific meeting.

- *Being responsive to conflicts and problems that evolve*: Guiding the group through difficulties that may come up and responding appropriately to destructive behavior in the group.

- *Learning about effective group leadership roles*: Participating in training opportunities that allow you to assess current skills and develop new ones.

- *Following up with members outside of the group*: Some members will appreciate opportunities to talk individually, while others may need referral for a counseling relationship. It is also the group leader's responsibility to help members transfer learning in the group to daily life.

- *Evaluating group progress*: Monitoring the group's capacity to achieve its purpose and make any changes to improve this process.

Let me emphasize how important your job description as a group leader is. It should outline your understanding of the specific responsibilities you have as a leader. If you don't have a job description, create one using the above information as a model. This will help you: 1) clarify the details of your role as a group leader; 2) help you get started in your new role; and 3) avoid unstated expectations. A "seat of the pants" orientation to group facilitation is dangerous and minimizes your responsibility as a leader. With appropriate preparation and training, your leadership role will be both satisfying and enjoyable.

Basic needs of grief support group members

- Each member must understand the purpose of the group.
- Each member must feel a sense of belonging and acceptance.
- Each member must feel understood.
- Each member must be aware of and respectful of the ground rules.
- Each member must feel encouraged to be an active participant in the group (while respecting "quiet" members).
- Each member must be able to see the face of other members (so arrange the seating appropriately).

Grief support group leader qualities

One of the foundations of good support group leadership is communication. To be helpful to your group members, you must communicate with them effectively and make them feel cared for.

We all have probably observed people whom we would call "natural helpers." Actually, the helping skills that seem so natural to them are more likely characteristics and qualities they have learned and developed over time. The most important quality is empathy, but there are others described below, as well. You, too, have the capacity to learn and make use of these helping qualities.

Empathy

Empathy is the ability to perceive another's experience and then—this is the key—communicate that perception back to the person. As a support group leader, I listen to you, and though I cannot experience your experience, I begin to have a mental picture of the essence of what you are describing.

Perhaps the most vital part of this characteristic is the ability to convey accurate empathy. Empathetic responsiveness requires the ability to go beyond factual detail and to become involved in the other person's feeling world, but always with the "as if" quality of taking another's role without personally experiencing what the other person experiences. (If you actually experienced the same emotions as the person you are trying to help, you would be over-involved.) To have empathy for another person does not constitute the direct expression of one's own feelings, but rather focuses exclusively on the feelings expressed by another, thereby conveying an understanding of them.

You know that empathy has been communicated when your group members feel that you "understand." As you know, to say simply "I understand how you feel" is not enough. The response goes beyond the "I understand how you feel" level to the "You really are feeling a sense of loss" level. In other words, empathy is communicated both verbally and nonverbally by understanding the person at the emotional level.

Respect

Respect is your ability to communicate your belief that everyone has the inherent capacity and right to choose and make decisions. Respect requires a nonpossessive caring for and affirmation of another person, respecting another's right to be who and what they are. This quality involves a receptive attitude that embraces the other person's feelings, opinions and uniqueness—even those radically different from your own.

So, the dimension of respect is communicated when support group members feel they have been allowed to give input without being pressured and when their opinions have been considered important. Remembering what the person has said, demonstrating sensitivity and courtesy, and showing respect for the person's feelings and beliefs are the essences of communicating respect.

Warmth and Caring

The warm and caring support group leader cultivates a sense of personal closeness, as opposed to professional distance, with group members. Showing you are warm and caring is particularly helpful in the early phases of building a helping relationship. The dimension of warmth is communicated primarily nonverbally. It often has to do with posture, affect, facial expression, and other nonverbal cues.

Warmth is a very powerful dimension in the helping process. In fact, when a discrepancy exists between verbal and nonverbal behavior, people almost always believe the nonverbal. A person's nonverbal behavior seldom lies. Consequently, a person who has excellent verbal communication skills, but lacks "warm" nonverbal behavior, would more than likely be perceived by group members as not helpful, indifferent, cold, or uncaring.

Genuineness

Genuineness is the ability to present oneself sincerely. As a support group leader, this is your ability to be freely yourself—without phoniness, role playing, or defensiveness. It's when your outer words and behaviors match your inner feelings.

The dimension of genuineness involves disclosing how you really feel about an issue. One important caveat: try not to tell others how you feel too early because your opinion may interfere with their ability to open up and express their own unique and equally valid thoughts and feelings. Genuineness can be very helpful, but timing is important. You can earn the right to be genuine with others through first developing the relationship.

Grief support group leader skills

In addition to the innate and learned grief support group leader qualities described above, there are a number of skills for you to learn and practice if you are to be the most effective grief support group leader you can be. It is my bias that the skills or techniques that are most useful evolve out of the work of the members and are specific to the unique meeting. In other words, at any given meeting the members will 'teach you" what skills will be needed.

Instead of using skills to "make something happen," use them to elaborate on what is already happening. Skills are means, not ends. In using skills, you always want to keep clearly in mind the primary purposes of your group. The use of specific skills should also be dependent on the population you are working with (support versus therapy group) and the unique personality of the individual group member (e.g., some members can tolerate or even seek confrontation while others cannot). Of course, cultural influences must also be respected whenever you use specific skills.

It's also very important that you find an experienced mentor to teach you these skills and provide you with supervision early on. Better yet, plan to attend a training on group process from an experienced group facilitator. This is just an introductory summary. You will need a mentor to help you develop these group skills over time.

Skill	Group Members' Response	Outcome Expected
Attending: Listening, giving attention to each person.	Communicate that you are listening; makes them aware of your concern.	Helps build the relationship; enhances trust.
Paraphrasing: Restating the person's basic message in similar, but fewer, words.	Feels supported and really heard, accepted.	Creates clearer self-perception.
Clarifying: Bringing vague content into clearer focus.	Clears up vague and confusing messages.	Clearer statements and increased understanding.
Perception checking: Asking for feedback about the accuracy of your listening: "Is that right?"	Allows person to feel accurately understood.	Quickly clears up any confusing communication.
Leading: Anticipating where the member is going and offering an encouraging remark.	Allows members to explore in a direction they need to discuss.	Encourages members to be responsible for direction of the interaction.

Skill	Group Members' Response	Outcome Expected
Encouraging description and exploration: Allowing for more depth in communication or reflection on experiences: "What was that like for you when Mary said that to you?"	Elaborates on her experience: "I was angry."	Member moves to greater depth of experience (must be well-timed and paced).
Providing information: "The purpose of this activity is…"	Assists in understanding of the "why" of doing an activity.	Leaders and members increase trust with each other when they know the why of the activities.
Focusing: Identifying a single topic to concentrate on: "Maybe we could talk more about your friend's response to your sadness."	Channels thinking and feeling about a topic of individual and group concern.	Increases members' understanding of one area before moving to another topic.
Allowing for consensual validation: Seeking a mutual (group) understanding of what is being said. "I've seen a lot of progress in you in that area. I wonder what other changes group members have seen in you?"	Invites group members to share observations of a particular member and offer support and encouragement.	Individual members learn how others perceive them. Empowers members who offer supportive observations.

Skill	Group Members' Response	Outcome Expected
Reflecting feelings: Expressing in fresh words the essential feelings, stated or implied, of the person.	Helps the member and others to bring feelings into clearer awareness.	Gives the member the message that you and the group accept his or her feelings.
Making observations: "John, I notice you seem so much more at peace with yourself than when we first began to meet as a group."	Member has something to respond to: "Yes, I am more at peace with myself."	Leader and members place attention on significant observations and can then explain.
Providing acknowledgment: "Sue, you look like you really relate to that. Does that fit with your experience?"	Members feels acknowledged and valued.	Leader models the need to acknowledge nonverbal forms of communication.
Nonjudgmental acceptance: "Bill, it sounds like you are not sure you want to be here."(tone is important)	Feels understood without fear of being attacked.	Members learn any thought can be expressed and talked about in the group.
Encouraging comparison: Asking members to contrast their experiences with others in the group. "How have others of us responded to this problem?"	Members share their ways of responding to a similar problem.	Greater insight of all members results from shared commonalities and differences. Learn alternative responses to problems, concerns.

Skill	Group Members' Response	Outcome Expected
Confronting: A leader response that helps a member explore what he or she wants to avoid: "I hear you say you have no support, yet you have given me a number of examples of how people around you give you support."	Assists the member in achievement of congruency (what they say and how they behave corresponds).	Creates a clearer self-perception and allows for greater self-exploration.
Summarizing: A method of tying together several ideas and feelings at the end of a discussion or group session: "As a group, we seemed to discuss several areas of concern today…"	The leader and members are able to recall important learnings or self-discoveries, provides a sense of progress toward healing.	Results in enhanced understanding and self-awareness; results in better understanding of group process.

Building trust

As a responsible leader, you will need to work on not only the qualities and skills I've set forth in this chapter. You will also need to be sensitive to the need to consciously create conditions for mutual trust to grow within the group.

One important way is by facilitating the honoring of stories. It is through the personal experiences of the members that people do the "work of mourning," and, as they do the work, mutual empathy and trust naturally build over time. The more time you allow for sharing stories, the deeper the expression of feelings will be, and the more rapidly your group's trust, relationships, and sense of community will grow.

Naturally, as trust builds, members feel more comfortable expressing a multitude of thoughts and feelings. In the beginning, participants tend to express "safer" feelings, but as trust increases, they often share more vulnerable feelings such as fear, helplessness, and anger. Obviously, as participants take greater risks in expressing themselves and continue to experience compassion and empathy from other members as well as you, the leader, community grows.

Do remember that as you lead grief groups in "honoring stories," personal sharing may be difficult for some members. Effective leadership means never forcing participation but encouraging and supporting participation.

You also build trust by providing a "safe place" for the expression of grief (mourning). To create an atmosphere for authentic mourning, encourage and support group members when they respond in compassionate ways to one another. As the group members witness the support in action from you and fellow members, they will come to realize that this group is a place in which they can honestly express what is going on with their grief.

Model for participants that it is not their responsibility to solve each other's problems but instead to support one another as they encounter the wilderness of grief. As participants realize they can express their grief without others giving unsolicited advice, they are more likely to trust each other and the group process.

And finally, to maintain trust, don't hesitate to revisit group ground rules when necessary. This is particularly true when it comes to confidentiality. Sound leadership requires that you make sure that participants understand how important it is not to repeat to others what group members express in the group. Model it, revisit the ground rules from time to time, and emphasize the importance of it. Without confidentiality, you have no trust.

Support Group Red Flags
Indications that trust may be lacking in a grief support group

The following symptoms may indicate that your group members haven't built enough trust among each other to make the group effective:

- A general unwillingness to contribute to the group.
- Long-winded expressions by only a few members.
- A tendency to focus on others instead of oneself.
- A belief by some members that the group cannot help them.

Can you think of any other indications that trust is lacking?

Suggestions for leading discussion

As group leader, your role is to facilitate—which literally means to "make easier"— purposeful discussion about the grief journeys of group members. This is a task that will require some planning and forethought on your part. Consider the following suggestions:

- **Plan each session**
  Write down your goals and expectations for each group meeting. For example, your objective in the first session may simply be to get to know each other. How will you accomplish this? In addition to letting members tell their stories, you may plan one or two group activities. You might also use music and appropriate readings as prompts for group discussion.

- **Have a routine**
  Especially when they're feeling vulnerable, people like the comfort of a routine. You might, for example, open each session with a short reading that you or another member has brought. Try to start each meeting slowly; participants may need a few minutes to "prepare themselves" before they can confront their pain.

- **Remember you're leading**

  Allow yourself to be a contributing member of the group, especially if one reason you started the group was to help you heal. But don't forget your role and responsibilities as group leader, either.

- **Be sensitive to differences among members**

  As group leader, you are probably an outgoing person who feels comfortable sharing experiences in a group setting. Not all members will be so forthcoming, however. Don't force people to talk unless they're ready. On the other hand, you'll also need to be on the watch for the member who likes to talk and monopolizes the group's time.

A word of caution: there is a fine line between strong group leadership and strong-arming your group. While members will appreciate your nurturing leadership, they will not appreciate too tight a rein on the group's interaction. (Always keep in mind what I said about "companioning" in the Introduction to this text. You must try to be both a companion and a leader at once!) Sometimes that means letting the group dynamic dictate what will happen next. Other times your "gentle firmness" will be welcomed as you guide the group in discussion.

Defining your leadership style

What kind of leader are you? Are you gregarious? Aggressive? Passive? Leaders I have found most effective in bereavement support groups lead unobtrusively but firmly. That is, they are warm and responsive at the same time they make others feel comfortable that someone is "in charge."

Two of the most important qualities in an effective group leader are: 1) flexibility; and 2) the ability to share authority. Being flexible is important because some meetings — especially as the group evolves — will naturally flow without much direction from you. That means that sometimes your meeting plans, no matter how well conceived, should be tossed out the window if the group dynamic takes everyone in a different direction. A good leader is never rigid.

The ability and willingness to share your role as leader is also very important. As the group evolves, one or two members will probably step forward as unofficial co-leaders. Encourage them. That may mean letting someone else lead a particular discussion or choose a particular reading. More important, though, it means letting the group dynamic—not your meeting plan—dictate the flow of each session when that dynamic is healthy and healing. The trick, of course, is to intervene and redirect when the dynamic is not healthy.

From Start to Finish
The Support Group's Five Developmental Phases

Why is it important to understand that bereavement support groups go through developmental phases? Because knowledge of these phases allows you to both respect and nurture the natural unfolding of the group's development. For example, if you were to expect in-depth self-evaluation of all members at the first meeting, you would not be respecting the reality that this kind of sharing generally does not happen until group trust has been established over time.

Groups tend to develop in a cyclical manner. This means that bereavement needs such as "the telling of the story" tend to be met again and again but at progressively deeper levels of meaning. Of course, individual group members have a vital influence on the process of group development; therefore the outline that follows is very theoretical.

Phase One: Warm-up and establishing of group purpose and limits

In the beginning of a support group, you can anticipate some normal anxiety about the general uncertainty of "what will happen here." Group members may be questioning their capacity to tolerate their own and others' pain. So, be aware that many group members will attend with a certain amount of hesitancy and some questions about whether or not they should even be here.

Among the questions that may go through their minds during this phase: Who else is in this group? How does their loss relate to mine? Will they understand me or judge me? Will I feel comfortable with these people? What will we talk about? Are there certain expectations the group will have of me? Will the leader make it "safe" for me to just be who I am? Will I have to talk, even if at times I don't want to? Can I trust these people?

Behaviorally, members will tend to reflect their unique personalities. Some will be more expressive, while others may be silent and withdrawn. This initial period of getting to know each other is critical for what will or will not follow.

The leader plays a critical role in making it safe during this initial phase of the group's development. Here the primary leadership roles include:

- clarifying the purpose of the group.
- gently encouraging each member to "tell his or her story" (who died, the nature of the death, why they are attending this group).
- assisting in the creation of ground rules for the group.
- modeling listening and helping everyone feel as if they belong here.
- facilitating details such as time of meetings, formats, etc.

Phase Two: Tentative self-disclosure and exploring group boundaries

This is the phase where members begin to learn what is expected to happen in the group. Every group has expectations (spoken or unspoken) about what will happen in the group meeting. Essentially, members are learning how to be participating members of the support group.

At this stage members begin to see themselves as a group and disclose more about themselves. Often this self-disclosure is rather tentative. It's as if the group is exploring whether it is safe to move to a deeper level of risk.

Differences in interpersonal styles and ways of coping with grief become more apparent during this phase, particularly among those members who are more independent and "take charge"-oriented with their grief journeys. Ann the Advice-Giver, Albert the Academic, and Molly the Missing (see pp. 70-75) may begin to display their behavioral ways of relating to the group.

Through increasing self-disclosure and the exploring of group norms or boundaries, members begin to learn more about each other, the leader, and themselves. During this phase the primary leadership roles include:

- continuing to model listening, openness, and caring.
- continuing to clarify member expectations of the group.
- reminding members of the ground rules established at the first meeting.
- providing a group format and facilitating any activities or homework to be discussed.
- being responsive to conflicts and problems that might evolve.

Phase Three: In-depth self-exploration and encountering the pain of grief

As the group grows and develops, a subtle but important movement takes place. The group begins to move away from the initial discovery of the "why" of the group and toward an increasing involvement in the work of mourning. At this phase, the group has shifted from second to third gear and is beginning to develop group trust at a deeper level. A natural insider/outsider feeling often begins to develop and certain members may begin to express how important the group is to them. Now the group is feeling good about itself and members look forward to each meeting.

Informal co-leaders may begin to emerge; try not to let this pose a threat to the group or the designated leader (you!). A higher rate of interpersonal self-disclosure and in-depth self-expression is now taking place. Often, lots of memory work is done as members share the lives of the people who have died. Interactions among members become more intense and emotional.

At this point, you as leader may have to become more supportively confrontive with problem members who try to detour the group from its primary purposes. Also during this phase, group members may begin to work more actively on helping themselves and others learn new ways of coping with the absence of the person who died.

Leadership roles during this phase include:
- continuing to model listening, openness, and caring.
- being supportive of continued participation of group members.
- assisting the group in dealing with any conflicts and problems that might evolve.
- making appropriate adjustments to content and format for improvement of the group.
- allowing and encouraging the group to be more self-responsible.

Phase Four: Commitment to continued healing and growth

During this phase, many members begin to ask for and reach out to others for mutual help and support. The group ambiance takes on a more relaxed tone. Members feel safe and "at home" in the group.

While you should not withdraw as leader, you should be able to share more and more responsibility with group members. You will notice group members modeling empathetic caring responses and trying to crystallize for the group new insights into the grief journey.

Remember — not every group meeting will go smoothly. You will have good meetings, great meetings, some not-so-good meetings, and maybe even some bad meetings. Try using humor to acknowledge a bad meeting.

Phase Four is clearly the most valuable phase in the life of the bereavement support group. In some ways, if the prior phases have been reached, it's like the group is on autopilot. Earlier concerns and developmental phases have been achieved and the group is moving at a faster pace. Respect and trust levels are way up, which allows members to share what they need to share.

At this phase, the group process is typified by much more open-ended expression of thoughts and feelings. Activities you have planned may need to be eliminated as the group seems to need more time for open discussion. By this time members are genuinely concerned about the well-being of other members.

Any missing members become a focus of discussion. Participants will want to know, "Why isn't Mary here tonight?"

Members also openly share their own encounters with grief during this phase. Participants take a more active role in their own healing and talk of how the group has helped them see themselves in an honest way. Group members will also often express their feelings of closeness to other members during this phase. In sum, the group's members have discovered their individual, personal grief journeys — thanks in large part to the interdependence of the group experience.

Primary leadership roles during this phase include:
- continuing to model listening, openness, and caring.
- being supportive of continued participation of group members.
- modeling of shared leadership principles.
- assisting the group in dealing with any conflicts and problems that might arise.
- making appropriate adjustments to content and format as the group evolves.

Phase Five: Preparation for and leaving the group

Obviously, the bereavement support group that progresses through the above four phases of development creates support and assists members in ways frequently lacking in our mourning-avoiding culture. Also obvious is that the kind of intimacy developed in the support group environment creates natural problems of separation when the group must come to an end.

Careful attention must be paid to the importance of this ending. After all, the group's closure is another loss for the group's members. Many grief support groups are so successful they resist ending. However, "graduation" from the support group is an important step toward reconciliation of the death of someone loved.

Expect a certain amount of ambiguity of feelings about the ending of the group. Ending may elicit withdrawal in some, sadness in others, and happiness in yet others. A theme of general optimism and feelings of progress and healing should override these natural feelings of loss. As group leader, you will need to be sensitive to any and all feelings connected to members leaving the group.

Reflecting on and affirming the growth that has been experienced in the group is a vital part of this phase. One or possibly two meetings should be focused on saying goodbye to each other as a group and supporting hopes for continued healing of the wounds of grief. There will probably be both some tears and some laughter as the group moves toward graduation. Enjoy this and be proud that you have effectively and compassionately led this group toward reconciliation.

Primary leadership roles during this last phase include:
- Creating safe opportunities for members to say goodbye to each other and to the group
- Recognizing and understanding the dynamics that occur when a group begins to end
- Encouraging reflection on individual and group growth related to the grief journey
- Providing referral for additional resources to those in need.
- Conducting an evaluation of the group

A reminder: this five-phase, theoretical model will be influenced by the unique personalities of your group members as well as by your own leadership style. Some groups will naturally move more quickly through these phases than others. The most important thing you can do as group leader is to ask yourself how you can make it safe for these phases to evolve. If your group is not moving forward or seems to be stuck, try to discern why the members don't feel a sense of trust or safety.

Planning Your Meetings
The *Understanding Your Grief* Model

We have all heard that the three keys in real estate are location, location, and location. Well, the three keys to successful grief support groups are planning, planning, and planning.

The effective group leader is a prepared and well-trained group leader. I suggest you plan each meeting much in the same way teachers prepare lesson plans: with a flexible structure and a purposeful sequencing of activities. In other words, don't try to "wing it."

Through the years, I have found that groups that are closed-ended (meaning that the group will meet for a specific, finite number of weeks), education-based (meaning there are elements of learning about aspects of the grief journey) with open discussion (meaning that any educational period is followed by a dedicated time for open discussion and exploration) work very well. I then encourage people to graduate to more open-ended (meaning that group members come and go depending on their needs and that there is usually less-structured educational content) groups. The primary reason that I strongly suggest this is that so many people come to the grief journey and need some basic information (such as the misconceptions of grief, the unique influences on their experience, the central needs of mourning, etc.) to help them on their way into and through the wilderness.

Following is a model set of twelve meeting plans that interface with my books *Understanding Your Grief* and *The Understanding Your Grief Journal*. These meeting plans are only intended as suggested guidelines. Be creative and consider creating some of your own activities that you think serve the needs of your unique group.

My experience suggests that the format that follows encourages the members to actively participate in the hard work of mourning and provides them a comforting structure that promotes open exploration. (Of course, my hope is that it also helps you as a leader!)

Please note that during the first meeting, you should be prepared to pass out copies of *Understanding Your Grief* and the companion journal to all participants. If you order all the books at once from my Center for Loss, you will receive a discounted price, which you can then pass along to group members. (Call (970) 226-6050 or visit www.centerforloss.com to order.)

Between each session, group members will be asked to read a chapter from *Understanding Your Grief* and complete the corresponding journal chapter. This support group model works best if participants do indeed take the time and energy to fill out their journals as completely as possible. Not only does journaling provide them with a healthy way to mourn, it produces a record of their grief and their support group experience.

But not everyone is a journaler. Don't be surprised if at least one or two of your group members are reluctant to journal—perhaps even refusing to complete this part of the homework each week. You know what they say—you can lead a participant to the guided questions, but you can't make him write down the answers. So if one or more of your group members won't journal, that's OK. Just encourage them to read the text and at least read through and consider the journal questions. Alternatively, you could ask them to speak their responses into a tape recorder or type them into a computer. And try not to allow the non-journaler's laxity to influence the rest of the group; if others see that the journaling is "optional," they may be inclined to let it slip, as well. Keep reminding your group members of the value of the journaling process.

Support group meeting plan—Session One
Introduction to the Group

Introduction/Welcome

Welcome the participants to the meeting and provide a brief orientation to the purpose of the support group. The introduction and orientation could include comments such as the following (if you are using co-leaders, as I hope you are, you will of course say "we" instead of "I"):

- Thank you so much for coming to this group. I welcome each and every one of you. As you know, this group will be a combined education-support group. We will be using the books *Understanding Your Grief* and *The Understanding Your Grief Journal*. As the group leader, I believe you will find these resources to be supportive and bring you hope.
- Each of our meetings will last 90 minutes; we will meet every week for 12 weeks. The first half of each meeting will be a discussion based on some content from the books. The second half of each meeting will be left open for group sharing.
- At tonight's meeting, we will begin to get to know each other, distribute the books, and go over our group ground rules. Before we get started, does anyone have any questions or concerns? Again, thank each and every one of you for being here tonight.

Next, the facilitator (that's you!) will distribute a printed list of the group ground rules established prior to this first meeting. (See sample list of ground rules, p. 18.) The group will then review the ground rules and ask questions or share concerns. Your group may wish to make changes or additions to this list.

Following a review and discussion of the ground rules, you as facilitator can model introducing yourself. If you are also a bereaved person, you can share something about your own journey and explain why you are leading the support group. Then you can then invite others to do the same. Essentially, you are asking them to say who they are, who in their life has died, and a little bit about why they want to be in the group. Obviously, part of your role is to bring sensitivity and encouragement to the group members.

Acknowledge that participants can say as little or as much as they like. However, it is helpful to give some suggested timeframe for each person to talk: "Each of us will take five minutes or so." Trust in the process and don't panic when some members take more time than others. Some members may talk more initially out of anxiety, while others will appear withdrawn and may even have to pass.

Again, trust in the process. If a member feels the need to pause for a while, the group will understand. Tears need not be forced, but certainly will be accepted if they occur. If necessary, you may gently remind the group not to interrupt with questions or interpretations when members are first introducing themselves.

At this first meeting, the sharing process is an important initial step in creating a supportive, healing group experience. As people tell their stories, a powerful bonding often begins. Go slowly. As I always say, "There are no rewards for speed." Listen, learn, and heal.

At the conclusion of the group sharing, you will distribute copies of the two books (*Understanding Your Grief* and *The Understanding Your Grief Journal*) to each person. Explain to members that the first book is for reading and the journal is for expressing their thoughts and feelings about what they read. Explain that the books introduce the concept of the ten touchstones—or what the author (that's me!) refers to as "wisdom teachings"—that are essential physical, emotional, cognitive, social, and spiritual actions for you to take if your goal is to heal in grief and find continued meaning in life.

Homework:
Everyone is asked to read the Introduction to both resources and Touchstone One in *Understanding Your Grief* before the next meeting. Invite and encourage the members to complete the journal for these sections (through p. 16). Obviously, group members should be asked to come prepared to discuss the material and their reactions to what they have both read and written. Members also should be asked not to read ahead in the books; reading the primary book and completing the journal will be a group experience. Finally, each person should be asked to bring to the next meeting a photograph of the person who died. You can invite them to attach the photo to page five of the journal if they wish to (size may or may not allow this). The photos will be shared at the next meeting.

Again, thank everyone for being a vital part of this group and let them know you look forward to seeing them next week.

Session One Notes

_____

_____

_____

_____

_____

_____

_____

_____

_____

_____

_____

_____

_____

_____

_____

_____

_____

_____

_____

Support group meeting plan—Session Two

Introduction to the Texts and Touchstone One

I suggest that you start this meeting by having members share the photos they brought. As directed on page five of the journal, you might ask each of them to tell the name of the person who died, the group member's relationship to the person, and what this particular photo captures about the unique life and personality of the person who died. Obviously, this group sharing of photos helps group members get to know the people who died at the same time it helps the bereaved person begin the long, but necessary, process of acknowledging the death.

Following the photo sharing, you will lead a discussion of the reaction to the Introduction and Touchstone One. The bulk of the discussion will probably come from the facilitative journal questions outlined in Touchstone One of the journal.

You will probably find that there are too many questions in the journal section each week to go through them one by one during the meeting. Instead, I suggest you pick out three or four of the questions that best seem to address the needs of this unique group and lead a discussion about them. There will be time in the second half of the meeting for group members to talk about whatever they want to talk about, which might include some of the journal questions not covered in the first half of the meeting. Use these remaining questions to encourage open exploration, discussion, and group sharing.

Key topics (from the journal) for discussion:
- Setting your intention to heal
  You might consider asking each group member in turn to read what they have written in response to the journal question on p. 12. This can be a powerful motivational discussion that sets the tone for the healing to come.
- Going slow and being patient with yourself in grief
  On a chalkboard or flipchart, write down group member's brief comments about impatient thoughts they've had about their own grief. Then together brainstorm ways in which they could be more patient with themselves.

- **Shameful feelings about mourning**
  Ask group members if they've ever felt ashamed of their thoughts and feelings since the death.

Use your leadership qualities and skills to facilitate the discussion each and every week. Approximately the second half of this and every following session should be used for open-ended discussion. However—do remember that each group meeting will have its own unique tone and dynamic. Allow each meeting to flow naturally.

Homework:
For the next meeting, each participant should be asked to read Touchstone Two—Dispel the Misconceptions About Grief (pp. 21-34) and complete the companion journal section (pp. 17-36).

Session Two Notes

_____

_____

_____

_____

_____

_____

_____

_____

_____

_____

_____

Support group meeting plan—Session Three
Touchstone Two—Dispel the Misconceptions About Grief

After initial warm-up, I suggest that you lead an open discussion of the Misconceptions About Grief outlined in Touchstone Two. There is enough content here that discussion usually comes easily to members. They often like to give examples of how they have experienced these misconceptions in their own journeys.

Again, use the questions outlined in the journal to encourage open exploration, discussion, and group sharing. This journal chapter has many, many questions—too many to cover during group. Pick just a few and concentrate on those, then if there's time, continue discussion with more of the questions.

Key topics (from the journal) for discussion:
- **The difference between grief and mourning**
  On a chalkboard or flipchart, make two columns. Title one "Grief" and the other "Mourning." To make sure group members understand the difference between the two, and to help them focus on not only grieving but mourning their grief, field examples of grief and mourning and write them in the appropriate column. (For example, sadness would go under grief; crying would go under mourning.)
- **Having faith yet still mourning**
  Now might be a good time to open a discussion about the role of faith and spirituality in grief. Knowing a little bit about each member's religious and spiritual beliefs—and how those beliefs affect their grief—will help group members be respectful of each other's faith. (Of course, an important point here is also that having faith and mourning are not mutually exclusive.)
- **Secondary losses**
  When the person you love died, what did you lose besides his or her physical presence? Try having each group member write several things they lost on separate slips of paper (one per slip), then collect all the slips of paper in a bowl or basket and draw them out, one at a time, for discussion.

- "Getting over" grief
  In the book I say that you don't (cannot!) get over grief; rather you learn to reconcile yourself to it. How do your group members feel about the reality that they will never really "get over" their grief but will come to reconcile or integrate it? Discuss.

Remember—approximately the second half of this session can be used for open-ended discussion.

Homework:
For the next meeting, each participant should be asked to read Touchstone Three—Embrace the Uniqueness of Your Grief (pp. 35-46) and complete the companion journal section (pp. 37-64).

Session Three Notes

_____

_____

_____

_____

_____

_____

_____

_____

_____

_____

_____

_____

_____

Support group meeting plan—Session Four
Touchstone Three—Embrace the Uniqueness of Your Grief

After initial warm-up, I suggest that you lead a discussion of the unique influences on grief outlined in Touchstone Three. On a chalkboard or flipchart pages, write the 12 "Whys" listed in this chapter. (You might also include a 13th heading called "Other"; this creates a place for you to write down group responses that don't fit in one of the 12 "Whys.") Just by looking at the chalkboard, the group can then easily recall the 12 influences and explore the various questions related to them in their journals.

Time will probably not allow participants to explore each question under each "Why," so use your judgment in processing them. Depending on your group size, you may want to break into two groups. Your skills in group process are part of the art of leading this group and making decisions about how to best lead the meeting.

Key topics (from the journal) for discussion:
- **Your unique relationship to the person who died (Why #1)**
Try having the group members pair up (in groups of two) and tell each other about their special relationship with the person who died. They may want to refer to their journal pages 38-41 for direction during this activity. Then, after 20 minutes or so, bring everyone back together and have the paired members present to the group what they learned about the other person's special relationship with the person who died. Having someone else summarize and paraphrase what you have said helps you feel affirmed and listened to.
- **The circumstances of the death (Why #2)**
This can be a difficult topic for mourners, especially if the death was unexpected, premature, or violent. But it's helpful to talk about. Consider having each group member share whatever most concerns them or worries them about the circumstances of the death—whatever it is that their minds keep returning to and can't seem to integrate into their hearts and heads. Sometimes just saying these painful thoughts and feelings aloud renders them less powerful. Sometimes hearing that other people have similar thoughts and feelings helps tame them. And sometimes it's appropriate to discuss if there is anything to DO about these lingering concerns. For example, if a group member's mother died of cancer and the group member keeps focusing on the mother's pain during her last days, maybe it

would be helpful for the group member to visit her local hospice and talk to the hospice counselor or one of the nurses specifically about these feelings.

- **The people in your life (Why #4)**
  This activity helps mourners focus on who can help them with their grief. This is an important exercise because after group members leave your meeting, some of them may not know where to turn for support in the long week before the next group meeting. Ask: "Who makes you feel better when you're around them? Why?" Lead a discussion in which you begin to define the qualities of good grief helpers. Also ask: "Who makes you feel worse when you're around them? Why?"

The second half of this session can be used for open-ended discussion.

Homework:
For the next meeting, each participant should be asked to read Touchstone Four—Explore Your Feelings of Loss (pp. 47-68) and complete the companion journal section (pp. 65-80).

Session Four Notes

_____

_____

_____

_____

_____

_____

_____

_____

_____

_____

Support group meeting plan—Session Five
Touchstone Four—Explore Your Feelings of Loss

This meeting is about all the various feelings mourners have after the death of someone loved. As you know, these feelings can be all over the map. Some people feel angry, some feel numb, some feel relieved. Most people feel a combination of feelings, and these feelings change from day to day and week to week. Keep in mind as you lead this meeting that feelings are not good or bad: they just are. Model supportive, non-judgmental responses for the rest of the group.

A warm-up exercise for this meeting would be for each group member in turn to tell the group how they're feeling right now. You could start. For example: "I'm feeling frustrated because Jack's medical bills keep coming, even though he died last year."

After the warm-up, list the feelings described in Touchstone Four on the chalkboard or flipchart:

Shock (also numbness, denial, disbelief)
Disorganization (also confusion, searching, yearning)
Anxiety (also panic, fear)
Explosive emotions (anger, hate, blame, rage, jealousy, etc.)
Guilt and regret
Sadness and depression
Relief and release

You can then jump into a general discussion in which group members share the feelings they've had since the death.

Another way to broach this discussion would be to give each group member a small sticky-note tablet and have them write down the feelings they've had since the death, one per page. Then have them stick the sticky notes up and down their sleeves. You're having your group "wear their hearts on their sleeves"! That's a good thing, because it's a metaphor for healthy mourning (expressing your grief outside yourself)!

This can lead to a discussion that not only affirms the normalcy and naturalness of each of these feelings, but also encourages group members to EXPRESS these feelings in some way—to not only grieve, but to mourn.

If there's still time after members have shared their feelings of loss with each other, you might consider grouping people according to a dominant feeling expressed. For example, if Joe and Jill both talked about feeling angry, pair them up and let them talk about their anger together for a few minutes.

Finally, try to save the second half of this meeting for open discussion.

Important: Touchstone Four covers clinical depression. Even though you may not be a trained or licensed therapist, as group leader it is your responsibility to help identify group members who may be in need of additional help. If this discussion reveals signs of clinical depression or suicidal thoughts, wait until the end of the group meeting and ask to talk individually to the depressed group member. Talk to him or her about your concerns and offer to help link him or her with extra help. Then follow up outside of class!

Homework:
For the next meeting, each participant should be asked to read Touchstone Five—Recognize You Are Not Crazy (pp. 69-86) and complete the companion journal section (pp. 81-90). If they have a linking object (you'll probably need to explain what this is; see p. 78 in *Understanding Your Grief*), ask them to bring it to the next meeting for discussion.

Session Five Notes

_____

_____

_____

_____

_____

Support group meeting plan—Session Six
Touchstone Five—Recognize You Are Not Crazy

Am I going crazy? This is such a common question for mourners to ask. Some of your group members may even have posed that question to you by now. Of course, the answer is almost always no. Normal grief just feels like insanity sometimes.

Start off this meeting by having everyone show and talk about the linking objects they brought from home. People may have brought articles of clothing, trinkets, blankets, sporting goods—just about anything can be a linking object! Talk about why they are important to each group member and affirm how natural and healing it is to have linking objects near.

After the "show and tell," ask the group members to place their objects on a table at the front of the room. For the remainder of this meeting, those objects will be a visual reminder of the special people who died as well as a way to honor the losses.

Next comes a presentation of the "going crazy" experiences listed in Touchstone Five. You may want to write the following items on the chalkboard or flipchart:

Time Distortion	Self-Focus
Re-thinking and Re-telling the Story	Sudden Changes in Mood
Powerlessness and Helplessness	Grief Attacks/Griefbursts
Crying and Sobbing	Linking Objects
Identification Symptoms of Physical Illness	Suicidal Thoughts
Drugs, Alcohol, and Grief	Dreams
Mystical Experiences	Anniversary and Holiday Grief Occasions

This Touchstone, like many of the others, could spur a discussion that could last for hours. You must use your discretion about where to take this discussion. Your group members may also teach you where the discussion should lead. Be flexible and attentive to their needs above all.

You may find that the topic of dreams and mystical experiences is a good one to end with. While dreams about the person who died can sometimes be disturbing, they are often pleasant and reassuring. Mystical experiences also tend to be positive. Closing with this discussion may help group members leave this meeting feeling uplifted and hopeful.

Important: Touchstone Five covers the topic of suicidal thoughts. It is appropriate for you to devote a few minutes of this meeting to a discussion of suicidal thoughts. You might ask: Has anyone here had suicidal thoughts since the death? Tell us about them. Helping group members distinguish between normal, passive thoughts of one's own death and active suicidal plans may also be appropriate. Even though you may not be a trained or licensed therapist, as group leader it is your responsibility to help identify group members who may be in need of additional help. If this discussion reveals signs of active suicidal thoughts, wait until the end of the group meeting and ask to talk individually to the affected group member. Talk to him or her about your concerns and offer to help link him or her with extra help. Then follow up outside of class!

Homework:
For the next meeting, each participant should be asked to read Touchstone Six—Understand the Six Needs of Mourning (pp. 87-99) and complete the companion journal section (pp. 91-106).

Session Six Notes

_____

_____

_____

_____

Support group meeting plan—Session Seven

Touchstone Six—Understand the Six Needs of Mourning

Try starting this meeting by writing the six central needs of mourning on a chalkboard or flipchart. Each member can refer to the list as he or she talks about these central needs with the group.

The Six Needs of Mourning
 1. Accept the reality of the death.
 2. Let yourself feel the pain of the loss.
 3. Remember the person who died.
 4. Develop a new self-identity.
 5. Search for meaning.
 6. Let others help you—now and always.

The journal questions for Touchstone Six may help participants teach each other about how they are working on these needs. Again, invite but don't force anyone to talk. The other participants will listen and learn.

Some questions you might ask could be:
• Does one of these needs feel most prominent in your grief right now?
• Are you struggling with one of these needs more than the others?
• Did anyone write a letter to the person who died (journal p. 98) that they'd like to read aloud?
• How is your self-identity changing as a result of the death?
• What "why?" questions do you have about the death? (Field responses and write them on the board.)
• Did anyone write a prayer (journal p. 103) that they'd like to share with the group?
• How are you at accepting support from others?

If, after the group has had the opportunity to talk about the six central needs of mourning, one or more of the six needs has not been talked about, you may bring them up. Pay particular attention to the sixth need: to let others help you—now and always. Discussion about this need can once again emphasize that healing in grief is a process, not an event. Even after this group concludes, members will need continued support in doing the work of mourning.

It's also a good idea for you as group leader to reiterate and emphasize the concept of "dosing" yourself with the six needs of mourning. They are not needs that you can work on one at a time and complete, checking them off your list. You will always need to revisit the six needs, and, like grief itself, none will ever be totally "finished."

Remember to leave about half of the group time for open-ended discussion.

Homework:
For the next meeting, each participant should be asked to read Touchstone Seven—Nurture Yourself (pp. 101-123) and complete the companion journal (pp. 107-118). Also ask each group member to jot down one self-care tip—one they actually use themselves and that works for them—and bring it to the next meeting. They'll be asked to share their tip with everyone during Session Eight.

Session Seven Notes

Support group meeting plan—Session Eight
Touchstone Seven—Nurture Yourself

Try opening this meeting with a presentation of the self-care tips brought by the group members. One by one, go around the room and have each person present their self-care tip and how it has helped them during their grief journeys.

As group facilitator, one of your tasks is to emphasize how important good self-care is during a time of grief. Good self-care, in all of the five realms mentioned in this chapter, lays the foundation for any healing to come. For example, if you're not taking care of yourself physically, it's easy to see how your physical complaints (illness, pain, etc.) could distract you from—or seem to supercede—your grief. Or if you're not meeting your social needs, you're probably not getting the necessary outside support. This Touchstone is an important one because without it, all the others will fail.

Next, write the Five Realms of Nurturing Yourself across the chalkboard or on separate pages on the flipchart:

Physical   Emotional   Cognitive   Social   Spiritual

Divide your group members into five smaller groups and assign each group one of the Five Realms. Ask each group to come up with a list of doable, practical ways that mourners could nurture themselves in their assigned realm. The litmus test for an idea to make it on the list is the question: Would I actually try this? If the answer is yes, put your idea on the list. If the answer is…well, probably not…don't put it on the list. The lists should also include ideas group members themselves have actually used and benefited from.

After each small group has had 20 minutes or so to generate their lists, have them present them to the group at large. Add ideas that other group participants vocalize during this presentation. (You might consider collecting all the tips generated tonight and then typing them up to distribute to the group at the next meeting.)

Additional discussion points can come from the journal questions for Touchstone Seven. Some questions you might ask could be:

• How is your body responding to your grief?
• Did anyone draw a grief map (journal p. 112) that they'd like to share with the group?
• What gives you pleasure and joy in your life?
• Did anyone make a list of their blessings (journal p. 114) that they'd like to share with the group?
• Have your friendships or your social circle changed since the death?
• Do you believe in an afterlife? If so, what is it like? (This may be a good question to end the evening on!)

Use the remainder of the meeting for open-ended discussion and sharing.

Homework:
For the next meeting, each participant should be asked to read Touchstone Eight—Reach Out for Help (pp. 125-143) and complete the companion journal section (pp. 119-128).

Session Eight Notes

_____

_____

_____

_____

_____

_____

_____

_____

_____

_____

Support group meeting plan—Session Nine
Touchstone Eight—Reach Out for Help

One definition of mourning is that it is the "shared social response" to grief. In other words, it is not only grief expressed privately outside oneself—by crying, journaling, or making art, it is also grief expressed publicly outside oneself—by talking to others, hugging and holding someone else, participating in a support group, etc.

Congratulate group members on being part of a grief support group. By coming to group meetings and sharing their thoughts and feelings with others, they are helping themselves achieve Touchstone Eight— reaching out for help.

Ask: Whom do you turn to for help? This discussion, in addition to the journaling they have already done on this topic, can help group members see that there are a number of people in their lives they can rely on for love and support. Sometimes group members just need a little encouragement accessing that support—opening up to the people who love them and being more forthcoming about their needs.

The "Rule of Thirds" (*Understanding Your Grief*, p. 127) is another good topic of conversation for this group meeting. The rule of thirds says that about one-third of the people in your life turn out to be good grief helpers, one-third are neutral, and the final third are toxic to the journey to healing. This is a good time and place for your group members to vent about this last third of the people in their lives! Encourage them to tell stories about how others have made them feel ashamed of their grief, judged them in negative ways, said hurtful things, etc. Then, counter this discussion with some exploration about the one-third that are the good grief helpers.

Note that this chapter also contains information on determining if you need professional help and signs of complicated grief. It's appropriate for you to bring up these topics during group discussion; it gives members who are having a particularly difficult time to consider whether they might need the additional support of a grief counselor.

Try reviewing the factors sometimes associated with complicated grief (an unnatural or untimely death, your personality, your relationship with the person who died, an inability to express your grief, and the use of drugs or alcohol) as well as the signs of complicated grief (postponing your grief, displacing your grief, replacing your grief, minimizing your grief, and somaticizing your grief). (See *Understanding Your Grief*, pp. 130-132.)

Ask group members if they personally relate to any of this information. If they see themselves as needing professional help or having complicated grief, offer to chat with them after class and help them decide if grief counseling might benefit them. Remind members—getting help is not a sign of weakness. Indeed, it is a sign of great strength.

Use the remainder of the meeting for open-ended discussion and sharing.

Finally, this chapter discusses the role of grief support groups. Here you are in a (I hope) thriving, healing group. By now the group dynamic should be strong and loyal. If you feel confident that your group is working well, a good closing activity might be to ask group members how they feel about the group and how it is helping them. If you think you might get more candid responses from an anonymous opportunity to talk about the group, pass out blank sheets of paper and ask each group member to write down one or two or three things about how he or she has found the group to be helpful. Give them five minutes to write, then collect the papers and you as leader can read them aloud.

Homework:
For the next meeting, participants should be asked to read Touchstone Nine—Seek Reconciliation, Not Resolution (pp. 145-152) and complete the companion journal section (pp. 129-134).

Session Nine Notes

_____

_____

_____

_____

Support group meeting plan—Session Ten
Touchstone Nine—Seek Reconciliation, Not Resolution

This is the meeting in which you review the concept of "reconciliation" in grief. I say that people don't "get over" or "recover from" their grief; instead they learn to "reconcile" themselves to it. In other words, they learn to accommodate the loss as part of who they are and proceed in their lives with meaning, purpose, and happiness.

You might open this meeting by writing on the chalkboard or flipchart the quote you'll find at the start of Touchstone Nine, on page 145 of *Understanding Your Grief*:

> *"Mourning never really ends. Only as time goes on, it erupts less frequently."*
> Anonymous

Talk about how group members feel about this quote. Do they agree with it? Have they found it to be true, either with this current loss or with past losses?

Speaking of past losses, now might also be a good time to encourage group members to share other important losses in their lives and how or if they came to reconcile themselves to those deaths. This conversation can serve as a reminder that just as they have survived loss before, they will survive it again.

The Signs of Reconciliation (*Understanding Your Grief*, p. 147) are another good topic from this chapter to discuss. In their journals on page 130, group members were asked to note the Signs they see in themselves right now. List the Signs on the chalkboard or flipchart and lead a discussion about reconciliation as they see it unfolding in themselves.

Keep in mind that depending on the unique losses, personalities, and life circumstances of your group members, as well as how much time has passed since the death, they may or may not be ready to discuss how or if they are moving toward reconciliation. For some, their grief may still be too new or too powerful for them to feel as if they are making any progress in their grief journeys. If this is the case in your group, it's OK to spend more of this meeting talking about their hopes for reconciliation or their frustrations or worries about never feeling better.

This chapter also explores the role of hope in healing. The main text tells you that living with hope is living in anticipation of what can be. The journal asks journalers if they have hope for their healing. How is hope playing a role in the grief of group members at this time? Lead a discussion about hope and its presence (or absence) in the hearts of group members today.

Use the remainder of the meeting for open-ended discussion and sharing.

Homework:
For the next meeting, participants should be asked to read Touchstone Ten—Appreciate Your Transformation (pp. 153-161) and complete the companion journal section (pp. 135-140).

Session Ten Notes

_____

_____

_____

_____

_____

_____

_____

_____

_____

_____

Support group meeting plan—Session Eleven
Touchstone Ten—Appreciate Your Transformation

The journey through grief is life-changing. When you leave the wilderness of your grief, you are simply not the same person you were when you entered the wilderness.

How are you changing as a result of this death? This is the topic of session eleven.

Some questions you might ask the group at this meeting include:
- How is your day-to-day life changing?
- How are your spiritual beliefs changing?
- How are your relationships with others changing?
- How are your values changing?

Don't forget to remind group members that while grief does often result in growth, it is not growth we masochistically go looking for. The death is not "justified" by the growth group members may describe. (You may want to spend a few minutes talking as a group about how everyone feels about the price they had to pay for this growth.)

This chapter also reviews the concept of purpose in life. Ask your group if they believe they have a purpose in life and if so, to please share it with the group. This will often lead to interesting and heartfelt discussions about goals for the future—which is an important topic for your group to review at this point. (After all, you only have one meeting left!) Given this opportunity, group members will often encourage one another in their intentions to do something about their newfound (or newly strengthened) purposes in life.

The other discussion-worthy topic explored in this chapter is that of your responsibility to live. I say that mourners have a responsibility to live and live purposefully on behalf of the person who died. This is a challenging statement and not everyone believes as I do.

Do your group members agree with this statement? If so, how does this responsibility affect their grief and their lives? If not, why not? Before they leave, ask group members to write a list of three things they could do on behalf of the person who died in the coming week. Ask them to report on those things at the next and final meeting.

Use the remainder of the meeting for open-ended discussion and sharing.

Keep in mind you should be helping members prepare to "graduate" from the group. This is your next-to-last meeting, and you will want to be conscious of the preparation for leave-taking in the group. Go back and re-read about the support group's developmental phases, looking specifically at Phase Five and your leadership roles.

Homework:
Group members have already completed reading *Understanding Your Grief* and filling out the companion journal. So there is no homework per se this week. You might consider if there is any activity you would like them to do in the coming week. (For example, you could ask group members to write a generic letter to new grief support group members. The next time you run a group, you could read these letters of encouragement and support as ice breakers at your first session.) It might also be a good idea to ask everyone to bring a special snack for the next meeting, since it is kind of a bon voyage party.

Do ask members to reflect on what the group experience has been like for them. You will commonly see some expressions of resistance to the reality that the group will end next week. Use your helping skills to help the group openly acknowledge any thoughts and feelings related to this reluctance.

Session Eleven Notes

_____

_____

_____

_____

Support group meeting plan—Session Twelve

Graduation

Graduation—it's always a bittersweet occasion. It's a time of ending as well as a time of new beginnings. For your grief support group members, it's a time to say thank you and goodbye, and re-emerge into their lives.

It's appropriate to remind your group that just because the support group is ending, it does NOT mean that their grief is. As you've no doubt discussed many times, grief never ends. And their need to mourn the death openly and honestly and continue to receive support from others certainly does not end after this final session. Be conscious of helping members identify additional sources of support to assist in the continued work of mourning. Flip to page 163 of *Understanding Your Grief* and remind everyone that a Directory of Organizations and Support Groups is printed there; some of your group members may be interested in getting involved with a national support group organization pertinent to their loss. Other members may need to talk out their plans to graduate to an open-ended support group or individual counseling.

This meeting is also about "graduation." Encourage each member to express what he or she feels was gained from this group experience. You may consider having each participant give a "verbal gift" to a fellow participant. This is a positive comment a member has observed about a fellow member during the support group. Each person is encouraged, but not forced, to participate in this verbal gift-giving.

As part of the graduation, you may also want to give certificates of support group completion to each member. (See p. 68 for a sample certificate. Feel free to creatively amend it to suit your needs, or contact my Center for Loss to receive a downloadable PDF you can print out.) Share food and drink and openly discuss whatever is on your group's minds and hearts.

Group members who want to stay in touch can be encouraged to share their phone numbers or e-mail addresses with others. If this hasn't already happened (it often does earlier in the group's natural cycle), you can take charge of this role by asking those who want to to write their names, phone numbers, and e-mail addresses on a piece of paper you'll pass around. After the meeting you'll photocopy the list and send it everyone who signed up.

Conclude this meeting by thanking everyone for attending the support group and reinforce that you hope each member has been helped in his or her healing journey. Remember to ask each member to complete and return the Support Group Evaluation Form (see p. 80). These will be invaluable in helping you plan for your future meetings.

Pat yourself on the back. You have just completed a successful grief support group!

Session Twelve Notes

_____

_____

_____

_____

_____

_____

_____

_____

_____

_____

_____

_____

_____

_____

Certificate of Support Group Participation

Be it known that on this day, _____ has completed the
Understanding Your Grief Support Group and has immersed him- or herself in the
Ten Essential Touchstones for finding hope and healing his or her heart:

Touchstone One—Open to the Presence of Your Loss
Touchstone Two—Dispel the Misconceptions About Grief
Touchstone Three—Embrace the Uniqueness of Your Grief
Touchstone Four—Explore Your Feelings of Loss
Touchstone Five—Recognize You Are Not Crazy
Touchstone Six—Understand the Six Needs of Mourning
Touchstone Seven—Nurture Yourself
Touchstone Eight—Reach Out for Help
Touchstone Nine—Seek Reconciliation, Not Resolution
Touchstone Ten—Appreciate Your Transformation

You have given and received support from fellow group members. Your presence and sharing
of your experience with loss have touched the lives of many, and for that we are grateful.
We wish you continued healing and hope for a renewed purposefulness and happiness in life.

_____
Group Facilitator

_____
Date

When Things Are Not Going Well
Responding to Problem Members

Murphy's Law ensures that no grief support group will run smoothly 100 percent of the time. Problems will arise, typically due to one of three reasons:

1) *Lack of leader preparation.* "Where are we supposed to meet?" "How long was this meeting supposed to last?" "I thought you were going to bring the name tags!" If administrative details aren't properly taken care of, group members will feel left in the lurch. On the other hand, problems can also arise when a leader is too controlling. In general, a lack of effective leadership skills can result in a number of negative consequences. Proper bereavement support group facilitator training will help you circumvent these problems.

2) *Discrepancies between group members' expectations and leader's expectations.* Each individual group member will have his or her own expectations for the group. The place to vocalize these various expectations is in your pre-screening process and during the drafting of the group ground rules. Without clarifying mutual expectations, the group is set up for failure.

3) *Individual participant problems.* Each person brings a unique personality and history to the group. No matter how well you pre-screen members, you will encounter challenging participants who will test your skills as a group leader. Effective intervention in these cases requires that you first establish a caring, trusting relationship between you and each group member. Sometimes group members will themselves intervene by confronting each other about problems arising in the group.

Following are descriptions of some of the more common challenging folks you're likely to encounter in your groups. I've suggested ways you might deal with each of them, but do keep in mind that confronting an individual member in front of the rest of the group is rarely a good idea. Instead, ask to meet with him or her individually after the meeting. And remember, even when you must confront, lead with your heart and with compassion. Usually, problem members are just teaching you about their personalities and their unique ways of interacting with others.

Amy the Absent

Amy is the group member who is there, but is not there. Sometimes this person is still in the initial shock wave from the death and is simply unable to speak. Amy may have tried to attend the support group too early in her grief journey, or she may just need the group to be patient and understanding. However, there are also Amys who consciously choose not to participate and interact with the group in passive-aggressive ways: "I'm here, but I don't plan to be a part of this group."

Appropriate ways to intervene: From the very first session on, make an effort to help everyone feel involved and a part of the group. Create safe ways to invite the Amys in, such as asking, "Amy, I'm wondering what your week has been like since we met last?" Making eye contact even when this person is quiet is also a way of engaging her and inviting her participation. If your Amy is an outright passive-aggressive, you may need to talk to her individually and explore whether the group can appropriately meet her needs at this time. You may discover that some people are just very shy, quiet, or overwhelmed — yet they perceive they are getting a lot out of the group experience. If you can sometimes help them let the group know this, the group can often embrace and accept them for the quiet people they are.

Ann the Advice-Giver

Even though you have created a ground rule that says, "Do not give advice unless it is asked for," you will, no doubt, have an Ann in one of your groups sometime. Ann is quick to inform others what they should do to solve problems. She may try to "take over" under the guise of being helpful.

Appropriate ways to intervene: Gently remind Ann of the ground rule about advice-giving or ask, "Did you feel that John needed you to tell him what to do about his concerns?" Obviously, the goal is to prevent advice-giving in your group unless it is asked for. We know that many mourners resent unsolicited advice.

Albert the Academic

Albert is the intellectual in the group and often likes to show off his huge knowledge base. He might quote a recent article he read or expose a little-known theory to explain his, or more likely someone else's, behavior. Analysis and interpretation are Albert's joys in life! There may be a condescending quality to his tone; generally he thinks he knows more than most anyone else in the group.

Appropriate ways to intervene: Initially, I often allow Albert's natural defense mechanism to help him ease into the group. However, when it becomes a consistent pattern, it can be destructive to the group. Therefore, I sometimes try saying things like, "Albert, you have really helped us understand what the articles say, but sometimes I wonder how you feel." Of course, he may lack insight, but it is worth a try. Sometimes when I know my relationship with Albert is strong I'll say, "Albert, I know that I sometimes have a tendency to intellectualize things that are painful for me. I wonder if you see that same tendency in yourself?"

Bob the Blamer

Bob is the participant who projects that other group members (or, other people in general) are the ones who cause his problems. This self-defeating thought pattern has often been a part of his coping mechanisms for some time. Bob often projects an accompanying sense that no one has ever understood him and no one ever will. This self-crippling stance wears thin very quickly with members who are trying to honestly look at themselves and sort out new directions in their lives.

Appropriate ways to intervene: Compassionately attempt to help Bob become more self-responsible and eliminate the tendency to blame. Well-timed, tentative comments like, "Bob, sometimes I'm struck by how often you find fault with others. I'm wondering what would happen for you if you looked inside yourself at times instead of outside?" A supportive confrontation like this has the potential of getting Bob more connected to himself and may help him make positive changes.

Charlene the Challenging

Charlene is the participant who likes to challenge the leader. She might accuse you of not knowing what you are doing, which in turn may cause you to question yourself. Charlene likes to put you on the spot and tries to make you look incompetent in the eyes of group. Her challenges are more often made in front of the group instead of privately.

Appropriate ways to intervene: Be certain you don't get defensive when the challenges come forth. This would be just what Charlene wants and would probably lead to more challenges. It is often appropriate to acknowledge her comment, but then offer to meet her after the group to better understand each other. While you may be tempted to initiate a dialogue that will prove your competence, resist the urge. The group will most often respect your decision to deflect the criticism and discuss the situation individually with Charlene.

Fred the Forced

Fred is the group member who is there because someone else wants him there. He has no intention of participating and feels he is being forced by a spouse or friend. He hopes everyone will forget he is present and will leave him alone. Fred rarely makes eye contact with anyone, particularly the group leader. If questioned or invited to participate, he often passes and looks put upon. If Fred is attending with his spouse or friend, he often defers questions to them.

Appropriate ways to intervene: Try to screen this person out in your pre-screening process because this person will be counterproductive if not outright damaging to the group. Once Fred is in the group, you can attempt to make him feel welcome and warmly invite his participation. However, if that doesn't work, the group will be well-served if you meet with Fred individually and explore the possibility of him leaving the group. You may also consider referring Fred to individual counseling, but he will usually resist this suggestion.

Holly the Holy Roller

Holly spends so much time talking about heaven that people wonder if her feet are on the ground! While faith values are very important and should be explored, the Hollys of the group often alienate other members by quoting scripture. Holly usually projects a lack of any personal problems and may perceive other members' pain as a "lack of faith."

Appropriate ways to intervene: Support that what works for one person may not work for another. You can accept how important Holly's faith is to her while also (with appropriate timing and pacing) helping her and the group acknowledge that having faith and mourning are not mutually exclusive. If Holly is advice-giving about the need for everyone to have faith like hers, you must gently remind her of the ground rules and redirect the group in ways supportive to everyone present.

Ivan the Interrupter

Ivan is the group member who, consciously or unconsciously, is always interrupting other people. He can't seem to keep his mouth shut. Other participants will begin to see it coming and will start hesitating to share for fear they will be interrupted. Ivan must be helped to control his interrupting tendencies or he will destroy the very heart of the group.

Appropriate ways to intervene: Gently remind Ivan of the "equal time" ground rule. When this fails, go to the next step: "Ivan, I notice that sometimes you have a tendency to interrupt the person who is talking. Are you aware of this?" You can then offer to help him when he does interrupt; it can often be done in good humor with excellent results.

Paul the Preacher

Paul has a lot in common with Holly, but he preaches about anything and everything. The group experience provides Paul with an audience. He may attempt to dominate the group as he tells the group what they should and should not do. He is usually very well-intentioned, but tends to wear thin with the group. He may seem overly rehearsed, as if he has preached his message many times.

Appropriate ways to intervene: Gently remind Paul of the "equal time" ground rule, as well as the "advice-giving" ground rule. You might express how his tendency to preach impacts you. Say, for example, "Sometimes when I listen to you, Paul, I wonder if you really want to hear what others think and feel." Again, this confrontation must be well-timed and intended to help him reflect on how he is impacting the group.

Ralph the Rambler

Ralph is a close cousin of Paul the Preacher — he just changes subjects more often. Ralph tends to bore the group as he rambles on, yet seems to say little of substance related to the needs of the group. He rarely completes his sentences in ways that allow others to talk; he just keeps running on and on and on. The group kind of lets out a silent groan as soon as Ralph utters his first words. Without a doubt, one rambling Ralph can ruin your group if you don't effectively intervene.

Appropriate ways to intervene: Once again, return to the ground rules related to "equal time." If this fails, step up your efforts to help Ralph by being supportively direct about his tendency to talk a lot. The group will often be able to help if you ask them if anyone was able to follow what Ralph just said. There is some risk in this approach in that a fellow group member may attack Ralph for rambling on all the time and saying little. Again, if all else fails, ask to speak with Ralph after the meeting and attempt to compassionately help him look at his rambling and become a more controlled contributor to the group.

Sarah the Socializer

Sarah's goal is to keep the group from getting too serious about anything. The problem here, of course, is that grief will bring about serious, thoughtful, painful discussions. Sarah may see the group as an opportunity to be with other people and socialize in a fun way. Obviously, her expectations are different than the group's. Sarah may laugh when everyone else is sad or make inappropriate comments to distract the group from the work at hand.

Appropriate ways to intervene: First, understand that many people protect themselves from getting hurt by trying to stay in a social mode or be humorous. Try well-timed, sensitive comments like, "I notice that sometimes you laugh when others are sad. How do you understand that about yourself?" Or, "When I see you laugh like that, I wonder what you are feeling?" Some Sarahs will lack insight into their use of socializing while others will appreciate your efforts to help them.

Wally the We-Sayer

Wally attempts to talk for everyone in the group or to be the group spokesperson. "We think we should . . ." is a common lead for this person. Wally assumes (and this is what creates problems) that everyone thinks and feels the same as he does. Allowing the "we" messages to continue often causes quieter members to give in to the "we talk" Wally espouses. Resentment can grow and some members will probably drop out and not even tell you why.

Appropriate ways to intervene: Ask Wally if he is speaking for every person in the group or ask the group if there is anyone who doesn't agree with Wally's statement. If it is healthy, your group will provide a safe atmosphere for people to express their unique personalities. Gently confronting Wally often helps achieve that goal.

Red Flags Suggesting Referral for Individual Counseling

There are some bereaved persons whose needs will be met more effectively in individual counseling or therapy. The following "red flags" should alert you to the need for making an appropriate referral.

- Persistent thoughts of suicide, expressions of serious suicide intent, or the development of a specific suicide plan
- Arriving at your group under the influence of alcohol or drugs
- Previous diagnosis of a serious mental health disorder
- Profound symptoms of anxiety or depression that interfere with the ability to do basic self-care
- Uncontrollable rage directed at others
- Physical harm to self or others
- Uncontrollable phobias, such as an inability to be by themselves at any time
- Characteristics of mourning (such as anger or guilt) that do not appear to change at all over a period of months

Note: the above list is not all-inclusive. You should use your good judgment as to whether or not a group member would benefit more from individual counseling than from a support group. It is also important for you as a group leader to realize that, even when you make a referral for individual counseling, the person may choose not to take your advice.

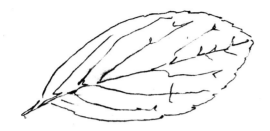

The Six Needs of Mourning
Evaluating your group's progress

"Progress" in grief is difficult to pinpoint. Grief is something we never truly get over; it is an ongoing, recursive process that unfolds over many, many weeks and years. So, if your 12-week support group is finishing up and you feel unable to quantify each member's progress, don't feel discouraged.

First, listen to what your heart tells you about the progress the group has made. Have you felt a growing sense of trust among members? Have members been able to share their experiences in a way they wouldn't have been able to elsewhere? Have you noticed particular members are able to open up more or cope better than they were when the group began? Have members thanked you for starting the group or shared with you how much it has helped them?

Next, ask group members for feedback in the form of an end-of-group evaluation sheet like the one on page 81. People often feel more comfortable expressing in writing what they can't bring themselves to say face-to-face.

Finally, consider the grief needs every mourner has and how the group has helped members work through those needs. Instead of the "stages of grief"—a term which makes grieving sound like a simple one, two, three process—I use the paradigm that follows.

The Mourner's Reconciliation Needs

Need 1. Acknowledge the reality of the death.

This need involves allowing mourners to gently confront the reality that someone loved has died and will not return. As members "re-tell the story," they move from head to heart in embracing the reality of the death. In fact, members acknowledge the reality of the death just by attending group meetings.

Need 2. Move toward the pain of the loss.

This need involves encouraging mourners to embrace all the thoughts and feelings that result from the death of someone loved. We all need permission to mourn. Sometimes what we need most from others is an awareness that it is OK to talk out our many thoughts and feelings, both positive and negative. Support groups provide a safe place in which to explore these thoughts and feelings.

Need 3. Convert the relationship with the person who died from one of presence to one of memory.

This need involves allowing and encouraging mourners to pursue a relationship of memory with the person who died. Memories that are precious, dreams reflecting the significance of the relationship, and living legacies are examples of some of the things that give testimony to a different form of a continued relationship. Support groups can help meet this need by encouraging:

- the sharing of memories, both spontaneous and through specially designed group exercises.
- the presentation of linking objects and photos.
- journal writing between group sessions.
- expressing hopes for memories that you wish could have been made, but never were.

My experience in learning from thousands of grieving people is that remembering makes hoping possible. The survivor's future becomes open to new experiences and relationships to the extent that past memories have been embraced.

Need 4. Develop a new self-identity.

Part of your self-identity comes from the relationships you have created with other people. When someone you care about dies, then, your self-identity is naturally affected. Your grief group members may have gone from being wives or husbands to widows or widowers, for example, or from being parents to bereaved parents.

Support groups help meet this need by allowing members to talk out their thoughts on these identity changes and explore them with others in similar situations. Many grieving people discover that as they work on this need, they ultimately come to discover some positive aspects of their changed self-identity.

Need 5. Search for meaning.

Your support group members will naturally ask many "Why?" questions about the deaths that have affected them. Why did this happen? Why now? Why in this way? Support groups help by providing a safe, nonjudgmental place in which to search for meaning.

With support and understanding, grieving people usually learn that human beings cannot have complete control over themselves and their world. They learn that faith and hope are central to finding meaning in whatever one does in this short life. And they learn a true appreciation for life and what it has to offer.

Need 6. Continue to receive support from others.

I have already pointed out that grief is an ongoing process that unfolds over the course of many weeks and years. So, while your support group may last for a finite number of weeks, your group members will need infinite support from others.

For some members, this may mean taking part in the same group again in the future. (You can help them decide if that is appropriate.) For others, it may mean continuing informal relationships with other group members; lifelong friendships often spring from support groups. Still others will leave your group ready to rely on other people and systems for support. In any case, it is a good idea for you to compile a list of community resources that people leaving your group can turn to in the months ahead.

Support Group Member Evaluation Form

What impact has this group experience had on your grief journey?

_____

_____

_____

What were the most valuable aspects of this group experience for you?

_____

_____

_____

What did you learn about "where you are" in your grief journey right now?

_____

_____

_____

What changes have you seen or experienced in yourself that you might be able to attribute at least partially to this group experience?

_____

_____

_____

_____

What are some of your perceptions of the group leader and his or her style of leadership?

_____

_____

_____

_____

Is there anything about this group and how it was conducted that you find yourself viewing negatively?

_____

_____

_____

_____

How did your participation in this group impact your significant relationships at home and with friends?

_____

_____

_____

_____

If you could describe in a sentence or two what this group has meant to you, what would you say?

_____

_____

_____

_____

Support Group Leader Self-Evaluation Form

How did you feel in leading this group?

_____

_____

_____

What were some of your initial impressions of this group? Did these initial impressions change over time? If so, how?

_____

_____

_____

Which, if any, members did you have more difficulty with than others? Do you have any sense of why this was?

_____

_____

_____

What skills did you use and what was the outcome?

_____

_____

_____

_____

What did you learn from this group?

_____

_____

_____

What turning points did you see occurring in this group?

_____

_____

_____

Is there anything about this group experience that you find yourself viewing negatively?

_____

_____

_____

What changes will you make for any future groups you lead?

_____

_____

_____

What additional areas of group training might you benefit from?

_____

_____

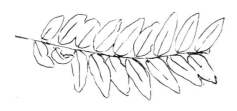

Putting Yourself First
Caring for the Caregiver

Like you, I'm proud of the work I do with bereaved people. At the same time, I've discovered that good self-care is essential to truly "being present" to those I wish to help. This is the caregiver's conundrum: How do we care well for others while at the same time caring well for ourselves? Perhaps, like me, you are aware that you may be good at meeting the needs of everyone else, but tend to ignore or minimize your own need for self-care. If so, this chapter should be of help to you!

So Why is Excellent Self-Care Essential?

For caregivers to the bereaved, good self-care is critical for at least three major reasons. First and most important, we owe it to ourselves and our families to lead joyful, whole lives. While caring for your grief support group members is certainly rewarding, we cannot and should not expect our work to fulfill us completely.

Second, our work is draining—physically, emotionally, and spiritually. Assisting mourners, whether you are companioning them individually or in a support group format, is a demanding interpersonal process that requires much energy and focus. Whenever we attempt to respond to the needs of those in grief, chances are slim that we can (or should) avoid the stress of emotional involvement. Each day we open ourselves to caring about the bereaved and their personal life journeys. And genuinely caring about people and their families touches the depths of our hearts and souls. We need respite from such draining work.

And third, we owe it to those we help. My personal experience and observation suggest that good self-care is an essential foundation of caring for and meaningfully companioning the bereaved. They are sensitive to our ability to "be with" them. Poor self-care results in distraction from the helping relationship, and bereaved people often intuit when we are not physically, emotionally, and spiritually available to them.

Poor self-care can also cause caregivers to distance themselves from people's pain by trying to act like experts. Because many of us have been trained to remain professionally distant, we may stay aloof from the very people we are supposed to help. Generally, this is a projection of our own need to stay distant from the pain of others, as well as from our own life hurts. The "expert mode" is antithetical to compassionate care and can cause an irreparable rift between you and your support group members.

So, does this work have to be exhausting? Naturally draining, yes, but exhausting? I don't think so. Good helpers naturally focus outward, resulting in a drain on both head and heart! Of course, you will hear some people say, "If you do this kind of caregiving, you might as well resign yourself to eventually burning out." Again, I don't think so. The key is to practice daily, ongoing, nurturing self-care.

The following self-care guidelines are not intended to be cure-alls, nor will they be appropriate for everyone. Pick and choose those tips that you believe will be of help to you in your efforts to stay physically and emotionally healthy.

Remember, our attitudes about stress and fatigue in general sometimes make it difficult to make changes. However, one important point to remember is that with support and encouragement from others, most of us can learn to make positive changes in our attitudes and behaviors.

You might find it helpful to have a discussion among other grief caregivers about caregiver fatigue syndrome. Identify your own signs and symptoms of burnout. Discuss individual and group approaches to self-care that will help you enjoy both work and play.

The Joy of Mini-Vacations

What creative ideas can you come up with to renew yourself? Caregivers are notorious for helping others create self-care time while neglecting their own needs. Here are a few ideas to get you started. However, I encourage you to create your own list and pursue them.

- Schedule a massage with a professional massage therapist.
- Have a spiritual growth weekend. Retreat into nature. Plan some alone time.
- Go for a drive with no particular destination in mind. Explore the countryside, slow down and observe what you see.
- Treat yourself to a night in a hotel or bed and breakfast.
- Visit a museum or a zoo.
- Go for a hot air balloon ride.
- Take an afternoon off and go to the movies—maybe even a kid's movie!
- Go to a yard sale or auction.
- Go rollerskating or rollerblading with a friend!
- Enjoy a photographic retreat. Take your camera into nature and shoot away.
- Watch cartoons with a child.
- Visit a farmer's market and shop for fresh produce.
- Drop by a health food store and walk the aisles.
- Go dancing.
- Take a horseback ride.
- Plan a river-rafting trip.

What ideas can you come up with?

_____

_____

_____

_____

_____

_____

_____

_____

_____

_____

_____

_____

_____

_____

_____

_____

_____

_____

_____

_____

Remember Your Child-Like Self

Have you ever met the overly-serious caregiver who projects gloom and doom? Odds are they have forgotten the vitality and enthusiasm of their childhood years. Let's pause and recall some of the characteristics of childhood.

Children:
• are physically connected to the world around them.
• take risks.
• are open, enthusiastic learners.
• imagine and dream.
• are naturally curious.
• spontaneously laugh and smile a lot.
• are passionate and expressive.
• try new things when they get bored.
• rest when they need rest.
• try to have fun whenever they can.

So, have you "grown up" and forgotten about the joy of being a child? If so, you may have left behind some of the best self-care strategies ever. Think about the way healthy kids go about their day, then think about how you spend your day. Have you forgotten how vital fun is to life and living?

There is a well-established link between play and energy. Playing often can be a vital part of your self-care plan. Being grown-up doesn't mean always being serious. Most really successful people not only work hard, they also play hard. Childlike behavior generates joy, fun, and enthusiasm. Ask yourself: What can I do to stay in touch with my inner child?—then jot down a few ideas here:

_____

_____

_____

_____

_____

Work Smart, Not Hard

Many caregivers never had the opportunity to learn essential time-management skills that result in working smart, not hard. You may find the following helpful:

Create specific goals for personal and professional development. Parse your annual goals into monthly goals. Break up your weekly goals into daily goals. Ask yourself, "What do I want to accomplish this year, this month, this week, this day?" Planning each day can give you a road map to getting to your destination!

Do one thing at a time. Caregivers are notorious for trying to do and be all things to all people and all projects all the time. Quality always suffer when you try to do too many things at once.

End the day by planning for tomorrow's projects whenever possible. That way, you'll not only waste less time getting started the following morning, you'll arrive at work feeling more in control of the day ahead.

Protect yourself from constant interruptions. When you're working on a task, nothing will sabotage you more than interruptions. Block out the necessary time to complete tasks.

Work when you work best. We all have certain natural peak hours of performance. Pay attention to your inner clock. Are you a morning person or a night person? Does a brief nap recharge you?

Focus and reject. This is a reminder to stay focused on the task at hand. Learn to "switch off" those things that prevent you from accomplishing desired tasks. Sometimes this means delaying returning calls and email. If you always "stay available," you won't have time to accomplish what you may really want and need to.

When all else fails, retreat to a hideout. When working on project development, you may need to find a "Skinner Box": a place where you can hole up with no interruptions. Tell only those who truly need to know where you are. You'll be amazed at what you get done.

When you know your energy level is dropping, take a break. After a 10-minute walk or a short nap, you may be able to accomplish much more than you could have otherwise.

Delegate tasks whenever possible. Watch out for "busy work" that might be done more efficiently by someone else.

Throughout the day ask yourself, "What's the best use of my time right now?" Focus on those tasks that need to be done first. This requires discipline, but will pay many dividends.

Build Support Systems

Our work requires a natural outward focus: on the needs of those we attempt to help. Such demands can leave us feeling emotionally and spiritually drained. An important aspect of self-care is to allow us to have sounding boards for how this work impacts our lives.

What do support systems provide for us? Ideally, supportive colleagues and friends provide some of the following:

Unconditional acceptance and support. In other words, friendships and the need to be nurtured and understood ourselves.

Help with complicated situations. Assistance in ideas that serve to help us in our efforts to help the bereaved and their families.

Mentoring. Encouragement to continue to develop new tools to assist us in our work. Models that inspire us and remind us of the importance and value of our work.

Challenge. Encouragement to stretch ourselves beyond our current limits.

Referral. To have connection with additional resources for the people in your care. Good caregivers will recognize occasions when it is appropriate to refer those we work with to other, rich sources of support and counsel.

Ask yourself, can I seek support systems when I need to? Who are the people in my life that make up my support system? List five people you could turn to right now for support and nurturing.

_____

_____

_____

_____

_____

Are you involved in any relationships that are damaging to you? What would happen if you placed some boundaries on these relationships?

_____

_____

_____

_____

Review your current support system and make an honest assessment of how well it meets your needs. Identify areas where you could use some change.

_____

_____

_____

_____

_____

_____

Remember the Importance of "Spiritual Time"

I have found that nurturing my spirit is critical to my work as a bereavement caregiver. "Spiritual time" helps me combat fatigue, frustration, and life's disappointments. To be present to those I work with and to learn from those I companion, I must appreciate the beauty of life and living.

Spiritual, quiet moments or "downtime" (for me, often spent in nature) recharge my spiritual energy. While you may embrace your spirit differently than I do, I encourage you to ask yourself: How do I renew my spirit?

Some people do this through prayer and meditation. Others might do this by hiking, biking, running, or other forms of physical alone time. Obviously, there is no one right way to renew your spirit. But one reality is that to be present to others in healing ways, we must each find a way to massage our spirits.

I've always found profound meaning in the words of Carl Sandburg, who wrote the following:

> A man must get away
> now and then
> to experience loneliness.
>
> Only those who learn how
> to live in loneliness
> can come to know themselves
> and life.
>
> I go out there and walk
> and look at the trees and sky.
> I listen to the sounds of loneliness.
> I sit on a rock or stump
> and say to myself
> "Who are you Sandburg?
> Where have you been,
> and where are you going?"

So, I ask you to ask yourself: How do I keep my spirit alive? How do I listen to my heart? How do I appreciate the good, the beautiful, and the truthful in life?

_____

_____

_____

_____

_____

_____

Listen to Your Inner Voice

As a caregiver to the bereaved, you may at times become grief overloaded (too much death, grief, and loss in your day-to-day life). The natural demands of this kind of ministry can cause you to have tunnel vision about death and grief. For example, if your own child has a headache, you may immediately think brain tumor. If your partner complains of heartburn, you think heart attack.

I'll never forget the time I returned home from a three-day lecture series on childhood grief to find my office manager had scheduled the following day full of counseling a variety of bereaved persons and two dying children and their families. Sitting there looking at the schedule, my inner voice called out, "I cannot do any more sadness right now. I need and deserve a spirit break." So, I rescheduled all appointments for the day and instead went for a drive through nearby Rocky Mountain National Park. I returned home in the late afternoon and spent the remainder of the day playing with my children and being present to my wife.

Caregiving presents you with the gift of an enhanced awareness of the many tragedies that touch people's lives. Just as those you companion are changed by death, you are changed by their experiences as well. To embrace our deep appreciation for life and love we must stay grounded—and to do so means caring for ourselves as well as caring for others.

A Self-Care Manifesto for Bereavement Caregivers

We who care for the bereaved have a wondrous opportunity: to help others embrace and grow through grief—and to lead fuller, more deeply-lived lives ourselves because of this important ministry. But our work is draining—physically, emotionally, and spiritually. We must first care for ourselves if we want to care well for others. This manifesto is intended to empower you to practice good self-care.

1. **I deserve to lead a joyful, whole life.** No matter how much I love and value my work with the bereaved, my life is multi-faceted. My family, my friends, my other interests, and my spirituality also deserve my time and attention. *I* deserve my time and attention.
2. **My work does not define me.** I am a unique, worthy person outside my work life. While relationships can help me feel good about myself, they are not what is inside me. Sometimes I need to stop "doing" and instead focus on simply "being."
3. **I am not the only one who can help bereaved people.** When I feel indispensable, I tend to ignore my own needs. There are many talented caregivers in my community who can also help the bereaved.
4. **I must develop healthy eating, sleeping, and exercise patterns.** I am aware of the importance of these things for those I help, but I may neglect them myself. A well-balanced diet, adequate sleep, and regular exercise allow me to be the best I can be.

5. **If I've been over-involved in my caregiving for too long, I may have forgotten how to take care of myself.** I may need to rediscover ways of caring for and nurturing myself. I may need to relearn how to explore my own feelings instead of focusing on everybody else's.

6. **I must maintain boundaries in my helping relationships.** As a caregiver, I cannot avoid getting emotionally involved with bereaved people. Nor would I want to. Active empathy allows me to be a good companion to them. However, I must remember I am responsible *to* others, not *for* others.

7. **I am not perfect and I must not expect myself to be.** I often wish my helping efforts were always successful. But even when I offer compassionate, "on-target" help, the recipient of that help isn't always prepared to use it. And when I do make mistakes, I should see them as an integral part of learning and growth, not as measurements of my self-worth.

8. **I must practice effective time-management skills.** I must set practical goals for how I spend my time. I must also remember Pareto's principle: twenty percent of what I do nets eighty percent of my results.

9. **I must also practice setting limits and alleviating stresses I can do something about.** I must work to achieve a clear sense of expectations and set realistic deadlines. I should enjoy what I do accomplish in helping others but shouldn't berate myself for what is beyond me.

10. **I must listen to my inner voice.** As a caregiver to the bereaved, I will at times become grief over-loaded. When my inner voice begins to whisper its fatigue, I must listen carefully and allow myself some grief down-time.

11. **I should express the personal me in both my work and play.** I shouldn't be afraid to demonstrate my unique talents and abilities. I must also make time each day to remind myself of what is important to me. If I only had three months to live, what would I do?

12. **I am a spiritual being.** I must spend alone time focusing on self-understanding and self-love. To be present to those I work with and to learn from those I companion, I must appreciate the beauty of life and living. I must renew my spirit.

Beautiful color wallet cards of the Caregiver's Self-Care Manifesto are available from Companion Press for $15.00 for a packet of 50. Visit www.centerforloss to order.

A Final Word

With appropriate preparation and a compassionate heart, you can and will help many grieving people find hope for their healing in your grief support groups. They will be transformed. Transformation literally means an entire change in form.

Facilitating grief groups not only transforms members, it transforms leaders. Remember to honor your own transformation. You have likely grown in your own wisdom, your own understanding, and in your own compassion.

I wish you well, my friends.

Selected Reading List

The following resources may be helpful to you in your work with bereavement support groups. While this is not an exhaustive list, the books included are among those that best explain group process and leadership issues.

Grant, A.C. *The Healing Journey: Manual for a Grief Support Group.* Vista Publishing, 1995.

Johnson, D.W. and Johnson, F.P. *Joining Together: Group Theory and Group Skills.* Englewood Cliffs, N.J.: Prentice-Hall, 1987.

Lehmann, L. *Grief Support Group Curriculum.* Brunner-Routledge, 2001.

Miller, J. *Effective Support Groups.* Willowgreen Publishing, 1998.

Sarnoff Schiff, H. *The Support Group Manual: A Session-by-Session Guide.* Penguin USA, 1996.

Shaw, M.E. *Group Dynamics: The Psychology of Small Group Behavior.* New York: McGraw-Hill, 1981.

Smith, H. I. *Death and Grief: Healing Through Group Support.* Augsburg Fortress Publishers, 1997.

ALSO BY ALAN WOLFELT

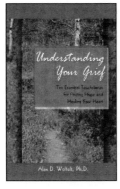

Understanding Your Grief
Ten Essential Touchstones for Finding Hope and Healing Your Heart

One of North America's leading grief educators, Dr. Alan Wolfelt has written many books about healing in grief. This book is his most comprehensive, covering the essential lessons that mourners have taught him in his three decades of working with the bereaved.

In compassionate, down-to-earth language, *Understanding Your Grief* describes ten touchstones—or trail markers—that are essential physical, emotional, cognitive, social, and spiritual signs for mourners to look for on their journey through grief.

The Ten Essential Touchstones:
1. Open to the presence of your loss.
2. Dispel misconceptions about grief.
3. Embrace the uniqueness of your grief.
4. Explore your feelings of loss.
5. Recognize you are not crazy.
6. Understand the six needs of mourning.
7. Nurture yourself.
8. Reach out for help.
9. Seek reconciliation, not resolution.
10. Appreciate your transformation.

The companion journal is an ideal place to write down your thoughts and feelings as you explore the ten essential touchstones.

ISBN 978-1-879651-35-7 • 176 pages • softcover • $14.95
(plus shipping and handling)

Companion
P R E S S

All Dr. Wolfelt's publications can be ordered by mail from:
Companion Press
3735 Broken Bow Road • Fort Collins, CO 80526
(970) 226-6050 • Fax 1-800-922-6051
www.centerforloss.com

ALSO BY ALAN WOLFELT

The Understanding Your Grief Journal
Exploring the Ten Essential Touchstones

Writing can be a very effective form of mourning, or expressing your grief outside yourself. And it is through mourning that you heal in grief.

The Understanding Your Grief Journal is a companion workbook to *Understanding Your Grief.* Designed to help mourners explore the many facets of their unique grief through journaling, this compassionate book interfaces with the ten essential touchstones. Throughout, journalers are asked specific questions about their own unique grief journeys as they relate to the touchstones and are provided with writing space for the many questions asked.

Purchased as a set together with *Understanding Your Grief,* this journal is a wonderful mourning tool and safe place for those in grief. It also makes an ideal grief support group workbook.

ISBN 978-1-879651-39-5 • 112 pages • softcover • $14.95
(plus additional shipping and handling)

Companion

All Dr. Wolfelt's publications can be ordered by mail from:
Companion Press
3735 Broken Bow Road • Fort Collins, CO 80526
(970) 226-6050 • Fax 1-800-922-6051
www.centerforloss.com

ALSO BY ALAN WOLFELT

BEREAVEMENT SUPPORT GROUP START-UP PACKAGE
Save 20%!

For bereavement support group leaders and participants, this package contains two copies of *The Understanding Your Grief Support Group Guide* and ten copies each of *Understanding Your Grief* and *The Understanding Your Grief Journal*. Subsequent orders of 10 or more copies of Understanding Your Grief and the journal receive a 15% discount.

$270.00 *(plus additional shipping and handling)*

Companion

All Dr. Wolfelt's publications can be ordered by mail from:
Companion Press
3735 Broken Bow Road • Fort Collins, CO 80526
(970) 226-6050 • Fax 1-800-922-6051
www.centerforloss.com